22/7/80 Lagers 26.25

THE TROUBLE MAKERS

THE TROUBLE MAKERS

DISSENT OVER FOREIGN POLICY
1792 – 1939

THE FORD LECTURES
DELIVERED IN THE UNIVERSITY OF OXFORD
IN HILARY TERM 1956

BY

A. J. P. TAYLOR, F.B.A.
Fellow of Magdalen College, Oxford

HAMISH HAMILTON
LONDON

First published in Great Britain, 1957
by Hamish Hamilton Ltd
90 *Great Russell Street London WC*1

Reprinted February 1964

SBN 241 90666 0

Printed in Great Britain by
Lowe and Brydone (Printers) Limited, London, N.W.10

TO
ALAN BULLOCK

CONTENTS

PREFACE

I GAVE the Ford Lectures before the University, and then a little shortened in the third programme of the B.B.C., with no written aid except the quotations. I have reconstructed them from memory complete with an occasional colloquialism and the snap endings. The text represents what I said a little more coherently; but still as lectures, not as a literary composition.

I have sometimes treated the Dissenters lightly, even critically. Nevertheless this books deals with the Englishmen whom I most revere. I hope that, if I had been their contemporary, I should have shared their outlook. I should not have been ashamed to have made their mistakes.

I owe a deep debt to the writers of theses, duly mentioned in the footnotes, whose labours lightened my own. I am grateful also to G. D. H. Cole, Henry Pelling, and Graham Hutton for the loan of material; and to M. R. D. Foot for criticizing my manuscript. A final word of thanks is due to my son, Sebastian Taylor, for sustaining me in the anxious half-hour before the lectures.

A.J.P.T.

I

THE RADICAL TRADITION

FOX, PAINE, AND COBBETT

I FIRST learnt that history was a living subject—exciting, important, controversial, and therefore often wrong—from H. G. Wells's *Outline of History*. One of the illustrations is called Tribal Gods of the nineteenth century, national symbols for which men would die. There they stand in a row: John Bull in masculine isolation, and four classically draped females —Britannia, Germania, la France, and Kathleen ni Houlihan. The four ladies look much alike—Kathleen ni Houlihan of course sadder than the others, Britannia perhaps more modest and matronly, France certainly the fullest in bosom.

The historian, particularly the historian of foreign policy, finds it hard to escape the Tribal Gods. We may remind ourselves over and over again that the foreign policy of a country is made by a few experts and a few rather less expert politicians. We may try to bring out the cross-currents which push foreign policy first in one direction, then in another. We may resist the assumption that governments are always in line with public opinion, and still more the assumption that public opinion, even if it can be ascertained, is ever in fact the opinion held by everyone in the country. But the Tribal Gods are always breaking in. We have to treat foreign policy as a block, a solid lump, if we are going to get through the story at all. We write 'the British' when we mean 'the few members of the Foreign Office who happened to concern themselves with this question'. Great Britain is made to move with the ponderous certainty of John Bull. In the end we build up a picture of an apostolic succession, in which statesmen

11

moving from one muddle to the next display 'the continuity of British foreign policy'.

'The British tradition'; 'the British way of life'; 'policy transcending party differences'—the incense of these phrases delights the nostrils of the Tribal Gods. I too have sent up my burnt offerings. These lectures are a gesture of repentance for having written recently a substantial volume of what I may venture to call 'respectable' diplomatic history. This time I shall emulate that slightly improper series of guide-books to capital cities called 'What isn't in Baedeker', and discuss aspects of British foreign policy that are left out of the official perorations. For the one continuous thing in British policy is not that it has been universally accepted but that there has always been disagreement, controversy about it.

This is not unique to Great Britain. Given a world of sovereign Powers, men will often disagree which partners to choose and which enemies. Mr. Kennan and Professor Morgenthau may complain that the foreign policy of a democracy is weak and confused, and may sigh for the resolute authoritarianism of the *ancien régime*. The advisers of absolute monarchs disputed just as much, and often with more disastrous results. Think for instance of the way in which Austria lost her supremacy in Germany simply because her statesmen could not make up their minds whether to go resolutely with Prussia or resolutely against her. Take the confusion of counsels which brought Russia to humiliation at the Congress of Berlin or, a generation later, to defeat in the Russo-Japanese war. We are apt to say that a foreign policy is successful only when the country, or at any rate the governing class, is united behind it. In reality, every line of policy is repudiated by a section, often by an influential section, of the country concerned. A foreign minister who waited until everyone agreed with him would have no foreign policy at all.

This practical disagreement, which partner to choose and which enemy, has gone on in Great Britain ever since she began to play a part in European affairs. And there are those who say that it is the only disagreement that matters, or indeed exists. When I mentioned my theme to a leading, though anonymous, authority on international affairs, he replied: 'The only problem in British policy for the last hundred years has been whether to oppose Germany or Russia.' Professor Butterfield, that Christian exponent of the Balance of Power, agrees with him: Christian statesmen, he thinks, should be as Machiavellian as their opponents. I started with much the same assumptions, merely thinking that it would be interesting to discuss some of the episodes in which foreign policy was most a matter of controversy. On further reflection it seemed to me that there was a more rewarding theme, at once narrower and wider: not just disagreement but dissent. I take the term from religious history simply because I can think of no better one. 'Radicalism' in foreign policy would do as well if the word 'radical' had not become associated with a wing of the Liberal party. At any rate, the analogy is close enough to illuminate what I have in mind. A conforming member of the Church of England can disagree with the Bishops and, I understand, often does. A Dissenter believes that Bishops should not exist. And so it has been with foreign policy in this country—and also in the United States: dissent is a quality peculiar to English-speaking peoples. A man can disagree with a particular line of British foreign policy, while still accepting its general assumptions. The Dissenter repudiates its aims, its methods, its principles. What is more, he claims to know better and to promote higher causes; he asserts a superiority, moral or intellectual. Sometimes the Dissenters have accused the Foreign Secretary and his advisers of ignorance, sometimes of corruption— usually class-selfishness rather than personal dishonesty. The Dissenters have differed widely in their practical conclusions. They have advocated everything from complete non-intervention to universal interference. But they have all been contemptuous of those in authority. It would be wrong to suggest —as exasperated members of 'the establishment' have often done—that the Dissenters cared nothing for the 'national interest'. On the contrary Dissenters have always claimed that the cause of Right (whatever that happened to be at the moment) was also a better way of securing peace, security, and even British predominance in the world. But these practical gains were a sort of bonus, deservedly accruing to the righteous.

Are they worth talking about at all? Were they merely dogmatic theorists, who knew nothing of the real world? The defenders of orthodox foreign policy have always thought so: an' most historians follow suit. Every historian loves the past or should do. If not, he has mistaken his vocation; but it is a short step from loving the past to regretting that it has ever changed. Conservatism is our greatest trade-risk; and we run psychoanalysts close in the belief that the only 'normal' people are those who cause no trouble either to themselves or anybody else. Historians who mention the Dissenters at all take *Hudibras* as their model: the Dissenter is a figure of fun, when not a scoundrel. Charles James Fox was a frivolous gambler, greedy for power, lazy, unprincipled; Bright and Cobden could think only of the cotton trade; John Morley was more ignorant than his cabinet colleagues—you would scratch your heads in vain if I recited some of their names; E. D. Morel was a German agent, Arthur Henderson an impractical dreamer; C. P. Scott and H. W. Massingham understood nothing of great affairs. In the favourite modern phrase, they were all 'rootless intellectuals', alien to the British way of life.

It will do no harm if I tilt the scales a bit the other way. Conformity may give you a quiet life; it may even bring you to a University Chair. But all change in history, all advance, comes from the nonconformists. If there had been no troublemakers, no Dissenters, we should still be living in caves. As to being 'rootless intellectuals', the Dissenters have been deeply English in blood and temperament—often far more so than their respectable critics. Paine, Cobbett, Bright, Hobson, Trevelyan—what names could be more redolent of our English past? One of the Dissenters found better words than mine:

How indeed, can I, any more than any of you be un-English and anti-national? Was I not born upon the same soil? Do I not come of the same English stock? Are not my family committed irrevocably to the fortunes of this country? Is not whatever property I may have depending as much as yours is depending upon the good government of our common fatherland? Then how shall any man dare to say to one of his countrymen, because he happens to hold a different opinion on questions of great public policy, that therefore he is un-English, and is to be condemned as anti-national?[1]

I recite these words with peculiar affection. The first advice on European history that I received at this University was to read the speech of John Bright from which they are taken. I thought little of his speech then. I have found it useful since.

However, it is unnecessary to take such high ground. The Dissenters existed: therefore they deserve to be put on record. They cannot be passed over by anyone who is studying British foreign policy in its official form; and they appear in all the books if only as 'noises off'. Time and again a Foreign Secretary has had to plead the Dissenters, usually as a convenient excuse. Foreign governments have been told that the British would gladly co-operate were it not for the impractical Radicals in the House of Commons. How would Salisbury have fended off Bismarck's promptings to join the Triple Alliance without Labouchere? How would Grey have resisted French pressure to turn the Entente into an alliance without the *Manchester Guardian* or checked Russia in Persia without Professor E. G. Browne? How would Baldwin and Eden have ratted on their obligations under the treaty of Locarno without the Labour party? Of course the permanent officials, and even the Foreign Secretary, resent the intrusion of amateurs in their 'mystery'. With Eyre Crowe, they 'deplore all public speeches on foreign affairs'. Yet, since the object of most diplomacy is to postpone decisions and to avoid action, the professionals should be grateful to those who strike the unwelcome weapons out of their hands. If Dissent did not exist, the Foreign Office would have to invent it.

[1] Speech at Birmingham, 29 October 1858.

Moreover—a point of special interest for those who are students of history, not its makers—though the Dissenters were always condemned at the time and are indeed usually condemned by historians, they are vindicated by posterity. Bryce said in 1899:

The imputation of being deficient in patriotism is always made against those who blame the diplomacy that brings on a war. It was made against Fox and Burke in the days of the American war. It was made against Bright and Cobden in the days of the Crimean war . . . it was made against Mr. Gladstone when he resisted the pro-Turkish policy of Lord Beaconsfield in 1876–8. Yet in all these instances it is now admitted that what was then the unpopular side had proved to be the right one.

Perhaps that is not quite correct: the Dissenters are still condemned, but their views are tacitly accepted. Macaulay said that Conservatism consisted in defending the Whig achievements of a previous generation; and this is true also of the conservatism of historians. Do you aspire to write the history books of fifty or a hundred years hence (if there are such things)? Then preach Radicalism now. Brougham said of the victors of 1814: 'They think only of dividing the spoils among themselves.' Now it is in every textbook. Look at the widespread belief that Stratford de Redcliffe provoked the Crimean war. It was launched by John Bright. Who do we read for the Eastern crisis of 1876–8? Seton-Watson, a thorough-going Gladstonian. Who laid down the interpretation of the first World war which was universally accepted between the wars and which is generally accepted even now? Lowes Dickinson, Brailsford, Bertrand Russell, Dr. G. P. Gooch—all members of the Union of Democratic Control, and the last a Radical member of parliament from 1906 to 1910. You can find their view fully-fledged in the pamphlets which the U.D.C. and the I.L.P. brought out immediately after the outbreak of war. Or take our present attitude to the origins of the second World war. All the authorities—Sir Lewis Namier, Mr. Wheeler-Bennett, Miss Wiskemann, Professor Toynbee—play the same tune: condemnation of

Munich, advocacy of alliance with Soviet Russia, the very
things preached by the Dissenting minority at the time. Turn
away from foreign policy for a moment. Look at that noble
monument of detached Tory scholarship, *The Structure of
Politics at the Accession of George III*. Its central doctrine is
that jobbery not ideas, places not principles, were the motive
force of politics. I used to puzzle where I had heard this before. Then I realized. It is a more scholarly presentation of
what Cobbett called THE THING. And how he was condemned for it!

I am certainly not going to waste my time arguing that
the Dissenters were right and conventional foreign policy
wrong. Our task as historians is to make past conflicts live
again; not to lament the verdict or to wish for a different
one. It bewildered me when my old master A. F. Přibram, a
very great historian, said in the nineteen-thirties: 'It is still
not decided whether the Habsburg monarchy could have
found a solution for its national problems.' How can we decide
about something that did not happen? Heaven knows, we
have difficulty enough in deciding what did happen. Events
decided that the Habsburgs had not found a solution for their
national problems; that is all we know or need to know.
Whenever I read the phrase: 'whether so-and-so acted
rightly must be left for historians to decide', I close the book;
the writer has moved from history to make-believe. Therefore I am not concerned to suggest that things would have
been better if the advice of the Dissenters had been taken. On
the other hand, the fact that it was not followed does not
prove them wrong.

Something more. Posterity does not merely adopt their
view of past events—though without acknowledgement; it
takes their line in the present. If you want to peer into the
future—and this is what many people study history for, very
mistakenly in my view—if you want to know what the foreign
policy of this country will be in twenty or thirty years' time,
find out what the Dissenting minority are saying now. The
policy being applied will be their policy—maybe at the wrong

time and in the wrong way, certainly to a chorus of Dissenting disapproval. Today's realism will appear tomorrow as shortsighted blundering. Today's idealism is the realism of the future. The attitude which Fox preached at the time of the great French Revolution—sympathy, conciliation, patience—was adopted, with great success and almost universal applause, towards the French revolutions of 1830 and 1848. Salisbury, a Conservative Prime Minister, endorsed Bright's condemnation of the Crimean war forty years afterwards, and refused to go on backing the wrong horse. The non-intervention of Bright and Cobden became a sacred cause for the National government at the time of the Spanish civil war. Gladstone advocated national states for the Balkans in 1878. The British government of 1918—a Coalition predominantly Conservative—promoted them at the expense of the Habsburg as well as of the Ottoman empire; and the most enthusiastic patron of this policy was Balfour, Salisbury's nephew. The appeasement of Germany which the Radicals had urged before 1914 was practised by the National government before the second World war with a devotion worthy of a better cause. More recently—six years ago—the British government joined in the Korean war with Conservative approval to vindicate the doctrine of collective security which the National government had betrayed in 1935. The abused Dissenters were entitled to a crow of triumph. Instead they remained out of line and preached peaceful co-existence. I myself quarrelled with the European service of the B.B.C. for wanting to say in July 1950: 'Appeasement is the noblest word in the diplomatic vocabulary.' Now 'live and let live' has become official policy; and only Dissenters doubt whether much good will come of amicable demonstrations towards the rulers of Soviet Russia.

I must say something about the problems of presenting my subject. The story of foreign policy has to be built up from hints and fragments even when you stick to the official line. It is rarely expressed in a formal treaty or alliance—and even these do not mean just what they say. You may complain that my story is scrappier still—negations to a theme which is itself never stated in full. There are few state-papers for Radical foreign policy. We have to piece its assumptions together from sentences in parliamentary speeches or newspaper articles; it is a stroke of luck when there is a relevant book or pamphlet. The Dissenters were critics by definition. They were more concerned to attack an existing policy than to state their alternative. But they usually had an alternative, even if it was that of not having a foreign policy; and I have tried to make the alternative clear, perhaps indeed too clear. I may sometimes give the impression of a systematic outlook, a conscious tradition, when there was little more than an automatic reaction to events. For if the orthodox diplomacy of the Balance of Power resembles a quadrille, the foreign policy of Dissent is more like Sir Roger de Coverley—a great deal of confused thumping and noise, which needs a charitable observer to discover the pattern.

I don't intend to discuss why men were Dissenters. To my mind Dissent is too normal and sensible to demand explanation. But I should like to discover why Dissent took a particular form. What background of knowledge did the Dissenters possess? Did they start with a fixed system, perhaps reading the speeches of their predecessors? You must remember that an M.P. calls it research when he opens an old volume of *Hansard*. Did the critics take the information provided by the foreign office in the Blue Books and turn it to a different purpose, as Bright, for example, did in the Crimean war? Or did they sometimes have their own sources of information, either as experts on some particular country, like innumerable Balkan enthusiasts and Wilfred Scawen Blunt in Egypt, or through channels which the official machinery did not recognize, such as the Labour party's connexion with the Socialist International? Sometimes the critics transcended Dissent and tried to run a rival foreign policy of their own— sending their representatives abroad, themselves negotiating with foreign rulers, insisting that they were the true voice of England. Charles James Fox was accused of doing this in

1791, when his friend Adair visited Catherine the Great at St. Petersburg. Roden Buxton, one-time adviser to the Labour party, put himself forward as the agent for 'secret diplomacy' with Hitler in 1939. The most striking instance is perhaps the line of the Labour movement in 1920, acting as mediator during the Russo-Polish war and actually proposing, though unsuccessfully, to send its own delegates to the peace negotiations at Riga.

There is one thing I must be careful about. I must not confuse Dissent with the party arguments between Liberals and Conservatives. These sometimes expressed real differences—more often than the Dissenters admitted. But they were differences, not Dissent—differences of tactics, not of fundamental strategy. The Dissenters were Radicals, not good party men who merely wanted an alternative government. They were however usually linked with the Liberal or later with the Labour party; and this produced confusion, especially when their party was out of office. For then its leaders claimed that they too were Dissenters, though of a moderate cast; and were themselves surprised when they became Bishops after all. Charles Fox was certainly a Dissenter during the war against revolutionary France; and after his death the Foxites tried to assume the same character. But they soon drifted back into the Whiggism of the seventeen-eighties when office was their only principle. During the Napoleonic wars they claimed to offer an alternative government; they had little in the way of an alternative policy. Yet, so far as there was a Dissenting group at all, it was bound to get tangled up with these Whig ambitions. Or again, at the other end of the story, the Labour party between the wars was both an alternative government and the nearest thing there has ever been to a party of Dissent. There were accusations from the one side of impractical idealism; from the other of betrayal. My narrative has got the strands confused here and there, as it was bound to do when trying to reproduce the historical record.

There is nothing more common than the lapsed Dissenter;

yet it would be wrong to speak of betrayal in any deliberate sense. Rather there lurks in nearly every politician an itch for Power. The dreary round of politics would be intolerable without this prize. There were very few who, like Bright, really did not enjoy Power at all; the only good thing about being in office, he once said, was receiving the salary.[1] Others wearied of mere denunciation; and were eager to show, no doubt on the highest principles, that they could do better. Cobden would have succumbed if he had lived longer; E. D. Morel aspired to the Foreign Office in 1924. The dominating figures—Fox, MacDonald, Gladstone—were deeply convinced that everything was wrong in the existing order, yet assumed unconsciously that the greatest of improvements would be to grasp Power themselves. From these men sprang the great 'betrayals'—betrayals at which they themselves were the most bewildered. It would be more convenient if some men devoted their lives to Dissent, and others sought Power; but things did not happen that way.

The true controversy of Dissent was therefore rarely with the Conservatives. They were so much beyond the pale, or rather so much inside it, as hardly to be worth arguing with. The serious argument went on within the Left, if I may slip into this Continental parlance—attacks on a Liberal or Labour government when it was in office; debate as to future policy when the party was in opposition. Palmerston, not Aberdeen, was the principal target both for the Chartists and for Bright and Cobden; Sir Edward Grey, not Lansdowne, was the Radical bye-word for secret diplomacy. The aim of the Dissenters in 1876–8 was to capture the Liberal party through the instrumentality of Gladstone, rather than to overthrow the Conservative government. Between the wars no Labour man doubted the wickedness of the Conservative or National governments: dispute centred on the question what the party would do when it won a majority. A man could be at one

---

[1] So Lord Eversley (Secretary at the Board of Trade under Bright) told F. W. Hirst. Hirst's diary, 9 April 1922, kindly communicated to me by Mr. A. F. Thompson.

moment a genuine Dissenter and at the next denounced by his brethren. Charles James Fox became a war minister in 1806; and, to compare small things with great, Arthur Ponsonby, a founder of the U.D.C., found its full force directed against him when he was Under-Secretary for foreign affairs in 1924.

On the other hand, office did not always wean a man from the Dissenting path, especially of course when it was an office remote from foreign affairs. Dissent within the Cabinet —as Winston Churchill and Lloyd George, for instance, led the opposition to the naval estimates in 1909—is a story of particular fascination; only dwarfed by the occasions when a Prime Minister dissented from his own Cabinet or, still more curious, tried to wreck his own work. It is a story that we cannot tell properly without penetrating Cabinet secrets— secrets which are guarded nowadays with what I cannot help feeling is an exaggerated pomposity and rigour. Things have come to a pretty pass when we cannot consult Gladstone's 'cabinet papers', really private jottings, without the permission of the Cabinet Office—an organization only created many years after his death. The absurd part of it is that these sacred documents, like most secret records, contain nothing startling, though much of interest to the historian; the secrecy is imposed solely to bolster up the self-importance of the civil servants who insist on it. There is no limit to my curiosity as a historian. I regard every official as my enemy; and it puzzles me that other historians do not feel the same. What is the British Academy good for if it does not resist this ridiculous ban? I hope to give you some instructive entertainment about the Cabinet despite it.

I know that I am running counter to the present fashion in history when I set out to discuss the ideas that men have held in the past. I remember well a series of broadcast talks on Human Nature in History, when distinguished historians told us that conscious thought counts for little. Men's prejudices and collective emotions, we heard, are all that matter; the less men think, the better for them and for everyone else. But men do think, you know. They persist in having ideas and ideals, despite the exhortations of Mr. Trevor-Roper and Professor Pares and Sir Lewis Namier. Historians have to take the past as they find it, not as they would like it to be; and our political past was shaped by the clash of argument as well as by family connexions and systems of land-tenure. If you find this too disturbing, bear with me at least in regarding the ideas of modern Dissenters with as much curiosity as those of medieval heretics.

I have more unfashionable behaviour to confess. I propose to tell a story and to tell it in chronological order. I shall start at some suitable point and shall jog on until my time gives out. History, to my mind, is distinguished from other social studies by the fact that in it things happen one after another. When I listen to my colleagues, from the experts in medieval administration to the indefatigable members of Nuffield College dissecting the facts of political life, I admire profoundly, but I cannot help murmuring with the needy knife-grinder: 'Story, God bless them, they have none to tell, sir!' But I do not mean to imply by this method that the Dissenters had a developing tradition or that each generation of them improved on its predecessors. Evolution works for sheep or roses or even for steam-engines; it does not work for men's ideas. These do not improve; they change. Dissenters sometimes evoked great names from the past, but they devised their policy anew in reaction to events. A hereditary Dissenter is almost as much a contradiction in terms as a hereditary bachelor. As a matter of fact, the children of Dissenters usually turn out impeccably Conservative. Cobbett's son, for example, was a delegate to the Chartist Convention of 1839; but he ended as a Conservative member of parliament, supporting Disraeli.

Nor shall I draw any moral which can be applied to foreign policy, or even to Dissent, at the present day. In my opinion we learn nothing from history except the infinite variety of men's behaviour. We study it, as we listen to music or read poetry, for pleasure, not for instruction. But there is one guiding thread which I may suggest in advance. Those who rejected official policy moved towards one of two extremes. Either they condemned action and so advocated non-intervention, sometimes in the practical form of advocating negotiations for peace in time of war; or they condemned inaction and so advocated war, for idealistic reasons, in time of peace. Both were Dissenting attitudes, both—confusingly—sometimes held by the same person. Both raised perplexing problems. The one: how could you oppose war and yet be a patriotic Englishman? The other: how could you advocate war and yet denounce the existing government? Dissenters did not always ignore these problems; they sometimes even strove to find solutions.

And now the practical question: where shall I begin? Englishmen have disputed over foreign policy ever since we had one. There were ideological differences in the early seventeenth century. Miss Wedgwood remarked recently that she understood better the Puritan desire to support the Protestant cause in the Thirty Years' war and the bitterness against James I's conciliation of Spain from having herself lived through the Spanish civil war and the controversies over appeasement. The present enables us to understand the past, not the other way round. Again, the Glorious Revolution was deeply concerned with questions of foreign policy; and the victory of William III meant also victory for the policy of war against France. In the eighteenth century, when all other differences between Whigs and Tories had perhaps disappeared—observe my modest caution—they still differed over foreign affairs. The Whigs stood for the Balance of Power and a policy of continental alliances; Toryism meant a vague detachment from Europe. When the Duke of Newcastle wanted to revive 'the old cause' after his dismissal in 1762, he could think of no better slogan than the Austrian alliance. 'Rule Britannia' was in origin a Tory song: it asserted that Great Britain should stick to naval supremacy and should leave the Continent alone—'Britannia rule the waves'. But I dare not venture on this theme. All the great authorities tell us that ideas and principles played no part in eighteenth-century politics—that was their virtue. And who am I to challenge them?

The war of American Independence certainly produced a true Dissenting resistance. I pass over it partly because I do not know enough about it, partly because the story deserves a series of lectures to itself. I am inclined to adopt a thought lent to me for this occasion by the Camden Professor of Ancient History that ancient history continues until 1789. At any rate, I cannot leave out Charles James Fox. He became the patron saint of later Radical critics. Cobden wrote in his pamphlet *1793 and 1853*:

> It is impossible to read the speeches of Fox, at this time, without feeling one's heart yearn with admiration and gratitude for the bold and resolute manner in which he opposed the war, never yielding and never repining, under the most discouraging defeats. . . . The annals of Parliament do not record a nobler struggle in a nobler cause.

In 1902, J. L. Hammond, then editor of the Radical *Speaker*, turned aside to write a life of Fox and claimed him virtually as the first pro-Boer:

> He was the first great Englishman, to extend to politics the doctrine of nationalism, to give a general application to the idea of national self-expression. . . . For him a national civilization was sacred because it represented the genius and the will of the people who made it.[1]

I have not managed to find these ideas in Fox's speeches, but perhaps that confirms my point. Forty years later, Hammond, as a leader-writer on the *Manchester Guardian*, was still quoting Fox and deducing from his speeches a foreign policy suited to the needs of the world after the second World war. I daresay, too, that Bertrand Russell, who was imprisoned during the first World war for his views on foreign policy and was still propounding his own line ten years after the second, may have heard from his grandfather descriptions of

[1] J. L. Hammond, *Charles James Fox*, p. 29

Fox's last speeches.[1] It is a further excuse, if any be needed, that Fox was the first Secretary of State for Foreign Affairs. For the rest of his life, whatever his supposed faults or failings, he spoke on foreign policy with unrivalled authority. This great man is passed over lightly by present historians; they attach more importance to his keeping a faro bank than to his principles. One day he will get the treatment he deserves.

I won't say much about the Ochakov affair in 1791. This was perhaps the last episode in the personal battle against Pitt and George III which Fox had been waging ever since 1784; and incidentally the one where he came nearest to success. He got back into tune with public opinion for once —both in the House of Commons and in the City. Pitt would have fallen if he had persisted in opposing Russia: even George III talked of accepting Fox as minister. But Fox's speeches illustrate no general principle; or, if they do, only the principle—pregnant with future controversy—that the House of Commons should determine foreign policy. Fox denounced 'the pernicious doctrine of confidence' which demanded that the House should swallow whatever ministers put before it: 'the duties of this House are, vigilance in preference to secrecy, deliberation in preference to dispatch.' We must look elsewhere for discussion of the Eastern question in moral terms. To Burke in the last speech which he made on the side of his old associates:

What had these worse than savages [the Turks] to do with the Powers of Europe, but to spread war, destruction and pestilence among them? . . . Any Christian Power was to be preferred to these destructive savages.

Or to Whitbread who held that Russian rule at Constantinople would conduce 'to the prosperity and happiness of the world'—'an event with which the paltry consideration of the nice adjustment of the balance in Europe was not to be put in competition'. The Ochakov crisis provokes one comment. In

[1] Fox was still a living symbol of Dissent in 1924, when Everyman's Library published his *Speeches during the Revolutionary War*, with an introduction by a prominent member of the U.D.C.

the last hundred and fifty years Dissent has prevented a determined government from going to war on two, or perhaps
three, occasions: Ochakov and the Russo-Polish war of 1920
are the two certain cases, February 1878 the more doubtful.
On each occasion the war prevented was war against Russia
—perhaps a coincidence, perhaps not.[1] At any rate the Ochakov
affair ran away to nothing. Pitt retreated; and Fox saw his
support in the lobbies sink from 162 to 116. It was small consolation that the Empress Catherine received his friend Adair or
placed his bust between those of Demosthenes and Cicero.

The war against revolutionary France which began early
in 1793 was altogether more significant: it was the crisis
which determined the rest of Fox's political life and gave
him his place in the Radical pantheon. Here at least his conduct cannot be explained by desire for office or power. If he
had succumbed to the anti-Jacobin panic and gone over to
government with the other Whigs, he would have become
Secretary of State. He would have run the war a great deal
better than Pitt—not difficult since the younger Pitt ranks
with the worst War Ministers in our history. Fox, not Pitt,
would have been 'the pilot who weathered the storm'. Such
a line never crossed his mind. Of course he remembered the
war of American Independence—how it had been popular at
the outset and how its failure had finally swept him into office;
and no doubt he hoped that a similar outcome would enable
him to strike a more lasting blow against royal power. Other
Dissenters have made the same calculation—Gladstone in the
great Eastern crisis of 1876–8, MacDonald in August 1914.
Even the Labour party owed its unexpected success in 1945
partly to confused recollections of the foreign policy it had
advocated—or been supposed to advocate—before 1939.

Moreover Fox held that Pitt's diplomacy was blundering
and faulty even when judged from the most orthodox stand-
point; and, reading his speeches a hundred and fifty years
later, it is difficult not to agree with him. Fox's speeches

[1] There has been another instance since these lectures were given, this
time not directed against Russia though it pretended to be.

between 1792 and 1797 were not acts of conscience, demon-strations—like Bright's on 31 March 1854—of superior vir-tue. They were practical advocacy, designed to show that the war could be ended by negotiation. After each speech, he divided the House; and he gave up the struggle in 1797 when he became convinced that he would never win over a majority. In the same way Cobden abandoned controversy during the Crimean war and Morley after August 1914. The practical nature of Fox's speeches makes them unsatisfactory for the historian in search of general principles; but it is not unusual. Dissenters have often been ready to challenge the apologists of official policy on their own ground, to show that policy was wrong even within its own terms of reference. Bright replied to Palmerston: 'I understand the Blue Books as well as he'—a justified claim; and Arthur Ponsonby, arguing for a negotiated peace during the first World war, quoted with effect words which Charles Grey, his direct ancestor, had spoken in 1796.

Fox did not only say that the war was a mistake; he used also the argument that the war would have evil consequences at home. He wrote to Grey about the renewal of war in 1802:

> Besides the mischiefs of war, in a constitutional view, of which we have had such ample experience, the certain misery it must occasion by the repetition of the Income Taxes, etc., etc., and the imminent danger of bankruptcy, a most material consideration in this case is the moral certainty of failing in our object, and of aggrandising France still more than we have done.[1]

Nevertheless, as a general rule, men hold that a war is un-necessary and that it must fail only when they are convinced that it is wrong. Fox was no exception. Like later Dissenters, he did not merely oppose the war; he sympathized with the other side. During one of the Ochakov debates he described the new government of France as 'the most stupendous and glorious edifice of liberty which had been erected on the foundation of human integrity in any time or country'.[2] He

---

[1] *Memorials and Correspondence*, iii, 373.   [2] *Speeches*, iv, 199.

never wavered from this opinion. When accused of welcoming the French victory at Valmy, he replied:

I freely confess that when I heard of the surrender or defeat of Dumourier . . . my spirits drooped, and I was dejected. . . . I saw in that conspiracy [of Austria and Prussia] not merely the ruin of liberty in France, but the ruin of liberty in England; the ruin of the liberty of man.[1]

He did not try to hide or to excuse the evils of the Terror, but 'the accursed confederacy of despots had given birth to all the suspicion and consequent massacres'.[2] 'Those who were concerned in framing the infamous manifestoes of the Duke of Brunswick, those who negotiated the treaty of Pillnitz, the impartial voice of posterity will pronounce to have been the principal authors of all those enormities which have afflicted humanity, and desolated Europe'.[3] Curiously enough, Pitt confirmed Fox's judgment. The Terror relaxed when the French armies were victorious; and Pitt found in this a justification of the war. As Fox remarked, Pitt's argument was 'that if they would permit him to go on in a system of disasters and defeats, it was incalculable what good it might do in France'.[4]

Fox denounced the idea of war as a moral crusade, risking 'the blood and treasure of this country in every quarrel and every change that ambition or accident might bring about in any part of the continent of Europe'. So too Bright opposed war for 'the liberties of Europe', and the Dissenters of 1917 objected to prolonging the war for the sake of the nationalities in Austria-Hungary. Fox also contrasted the virtues of the enemy with the wickedness of the allies, much like those who denounced the secret treaties in 1917. Here are the two arguments rolled into one. 'The hatred of vice is no just cause of war between nations. If it were, good God, with which of those powers with whom we are now combined against France should we be at peace?' In nearly every speech he pointed to the second partition of Poland. The British

[1] *Speeches*, iv, 447–9.   [2] *Speeches*, v, 472.
[3] *Speeches*, v, 156.   [4] *Speeches*, v, 370.

government had not protested, was indeed allied with the partitioning Powers. Ministers 'gave away Poland with as little compunction as honour'. How then could they claim moral virtue? Dissenters made much of Poland from Fox's day until this country went to war for her sake in 1939. Poland was the strongest factor in Radical agitation after 1830 and a powerful cause of the Crimean war. But it was always Poland as a weapon against some other country, whether Germany or Russia; not admiration of Poland for her own sake. This, I suppose, is what Mickiewicz meant when he called Poland 'the Christ among the nations'. More generally Fox hoped that when peace came, 'it will not be proposed on the dividing system', and that 'the interests of humanity as well as of kings, and that of every particular state will be consulted, and that tranquillity will be re-established on the broad basis of justice'.[1] Here were the texts for later Dissenting attacks on the treaties both of Vienna and of Versailles.

Fox was accused, as other opponents of war have been, of neglecting the security of the country. He replied that peace was the best security. If there must be war, he would rely on the Navy, like twentieth-century Radicals after him. He said in 1794: 'In our present circumstances, the neglect of building a single ship that could possibly be built, was a neglect highly criminal.'[2] This was a reversion to the old Tory line— a curious change of roles. He took up former Tory cries also when he denounced Pitt's policy of alliances and wanted Great Britain to rely on her own strength. Ostensibly he distrusted the constancy of the foreign powers. Really his dislike of them rested on principle—'this accursed conspiracy of despots' and 'detested league of kings'. He would have liked England to appear as the champion of freedom:

Cherish the spirit of freedom in the people of this country. Restore to them the right of popular discussion. . . . Instead of amusing them with panegyrics upon the form, allow them to possess the spirit of the old constitution of England; then you will

[1] *Speeches*, vi, 116.   [2] *Speeches*, v, 340.

indeed see the energy of the people of England. . . . These are your real resources; the rest are all imaginary.[1]

Why had the British government embarked on war at all? Fox held that ministers were acting to secure their places and to destroy liberty in this country. The war was promoted by a party 'who, at different times, under the appellation of High Churchmen, Jacobites, and Tories, had endeavoured to destroy the civil liberties of the country';[2]

Both the present and the American war were owing to a court party in this country, that hated the very name of liberty; and to an indifference, amounting to barbarity, in the minister, to the distresses of the people.[3]

Fox accused Pitt, in particular, of enjoying the glamour, the tinsel romance, of war. There is a splendid passage in which Fox answers the speech with which Pitt hailed the renewal of war in 1803:

When I hear all these fine and eloquent philippics, I cannot help recollecting what fruits such speeches have generally produced, and dreading the devastation and carnage which usually attend them. The right honourable gentleman, when he appears before us in all the gorgeous attire of his eloquence, reminds me of a story which is told of a barbarous prince of Morocco, a Muley Molock, or a Muley Ishmael, who never put on his gayest garments, or appeared in extraordinary pomp, but as a prelude to the murder of many of his subjects. Now, when I behold splendour much more bright, when I perceive the labours of an accomplished mind — when I listen to words so choice, and contemplate all the charms of his polished elocution, — it is well enough for me, sitting in this House, to enjoy the scene, but it gives me most gloomy tidings to convey to my constituents in the lobby.[4]

The mention of constituents is a reminder that Fox's opposition to the war was confined to the House of Commons. He held that the people had the right to resist Pitt's measures against their liberty; on one famous occasion he gave the defiant toast, 'Our Sovereign the People', and was struck off the Privy Council for it. But the people and popular agitators

---

[1] *Speeches*, vi, 227.   [2] *Speeches*, v, 312.
[3] *Speeches*, v, 339.   [4] *Speeches*, vi, 527.

remained remote from him. He read only the first part of the *Rights of Man* and pronounced it a libel, though not a seditious libel. If he had read on, he would have found in it views on foreign policy very like his own.

Though Tom Paine was once Foreign Secretary to the American Congress, he had little interest in the details of foreign affairs. Professor Feiling tells us that 'Paine had not a rudiment of English feeling, nor was he a thinker'.[1] This is a curious thing to say about a man of pure English blood and Quaker upbringing, author of one of the most famous books in the language, a book which can be read with undiminished excitement after a hundred and fifty years. Perhaps Professor Feiling thinks thàt 'English feeling' is a quality confined to the bureaucrats of our now-vanished Indian empire—or to the notorious plunderer, Warren Hastings. Paine defined in a few casual sentences the general principles of foreign policy which Dissenters were to display ever afterwards. It is discouraging to find the whole story worked out almost before it had started; discouraging, but not surprising. For *The Rights of Man* is in my opinion the greatest political disquisition written by an Englishman.

Paine's view of foreign affairs can be expressed in two sentences. Wars are caused by governments. Democracy will end them. 'Man is not the enemy of Man, but through the medium of a false system of government.'[2] Governments promote war 'as it easily furnishes the pretence of necessity for taxes and appointments to place and offices'—Bright and Cobden were to make good use of this idea. 'To establish any mode to abolish war, however advantageous it might be to Nations, would be to take from such Government the most lucrative of its branches.'[3] 'As a new system is now opening to the view of the world, the European courts are plotting to counteract it. . . . A common interest of courts is forming against the common interests of Man.'[4] The new system of

---

[1] Keith Feiling, *A History of England* (1950), p. 742.
[2] *Rights of Man*, i, 78.   [3] *Rights of Man*, i, 77.
[4] *Rights of Man*, ii, 50–1.

democracy would create an alliance of England, France, and the United States. This alliance would propose 'with effect, a limitation to, and a general dismantling of, all the navies of Europe'.[1] Then 'nations will become acquainted, and the animosities and the prejudices fomented by the intrigues and artifice of Courts will cease'.[2] These are now impeccably respectable sentiments, reiterated by the three Western Powers.

The Radicals of the day drew from Tom Paine the moral that foreign policy did not concern them. It was a conspiracy run by the old order and would disappear with the triumph of Radicalism—much in the spirit of Trotsky's remark on becoming Commissar for Foreign Affairs in 1917: 'I shall issue a few proclamations and then shut up shop.' Fox's withdrawal from parliament in 1797 pointed to the same conclusion. There was nothing to be done while the old order endured; and its overthrow would solve all foreign problems. Fox returned to the House of Commons in 1801 and welcomed the peace of Amiens as the justification of his prophecies. 'The triumph of the French Government over the English does in fact afford me a degree of pleasure which it is very difficult to disguise.'[3] He even imagined that his hopes for a better future were being fulfilled. 'If our two countries have liberal governments at the same time, the cause of the human race is won.' This sentence anticipated Radical foreign policy for a century afterwards; it had no relevance to the present, and Fox did little to put it into practice. He visited Paris after the peace of Amiens primarily to collect material for his history of England and had an interview with Bonaparte which does not seem to have gone beyond generalities.

The Napoleonic wars did not provoke a clear Dissenting reaction. When the war broke out, Fox criticized the retention of Malta which had provoked it and again argued that war was unnecessary. But the heart had gone out of his conviction; and there was a significant change of tone when he

[1] *Rights of Man*, ii, 87. [2] *Rights of Man*, ii, 88.
[3] *Memorials and Correspondence*, iii, 349.

wrote to Lord Holland: 'Next to peace, what I should least dislike would be a war in which Great Britain should have justice
on her side, but I despair even of that.'[1] His only important
speech in 1804 was on the conduct of the war, not on its
existence. He would have become a minister then but for the
objections of George III; and he became Foreign Secretary
in 1806 on the death of Pitt. During his few remaining months
of life he tried to put his earlier doctrines into practice and
negotiated for peace with Talleyrand. Nothing was accomplished; and he died with his mind unresolved—an advocate
of peace who might have become a great War Minister, an
advocate of freedom who left no answer what should be done
when Europe was really threatened by a tyrant.

Fox's death left the Whigs and even the Radicals at a
loss. They never escaped from it during the Napoleonic war.
Whitbread continued to bring forward resolutions in favour
of a negotiated peace similar to those which Fox had supported during the war against the French Revolution. Roscoe,
the Liverpool Whig, wrote pamphlets on the same line. But
Grey and the bulk of the Whig party backed the war, though
they asserted that the Tories ran it badly. A few Radicals—
Hazlitt in particular—continued to treat Napoleon as the
champion of freedom. Most Radicals voiced popular discon-
tent without formulating any foreign policy. Like Paine, they
regarded the war as one of Courts, not of Nations. Napoleon's
invasion of Spain gave an opening for a new approach. Here
was popular resistance to an aggressor, something which Dissenters might champion without violating their principles.
Horner, who had been very close to Fox, regretted that the
Whigs did not treat Spain as 'the turn of things in the contrary direction' and claim first place in opposing Napoleon.
Holland, Fox's nephew and 'young one', threw himself into
the Spanish war—at any rate to the extent of conducting
parties of Whigs round the battlefields. But there was nothing
serious behind it. The Peninsular war passed over without
any Dissenting reaction for or against it.

[1] *Memorials and Correspondence*, iii, 217.

The Foxite tradition revived when things began to go against Napoleon in 1813. The Whigs talked eagerly of a negotiated peace; and they suggested some of the things to negotiate about. Fox had pointed to the partitions of Poland as a reason for not co-operating with 'the confederacy of despots'; his heirs championed the Polish cause. Brougham was won for Poland by an emissary from Czartoryski. He wrote in his own name a pamphlet, *An Appeal to the Allies and the English Nation on Behalf of Poland*, and then reviewed it with anonymous enthusiasm in the *Edinburgh Review* —an admirable arrangement. Czartoryski wanted a Kingdom of Poland under the sovereignty of the tsar; and this was substantially achieved at the Congress of Vienna. English historians show an odd persistence in getting things wrong about Poland, and nowhere more so than on this occasion. They imply that Castlereagh was defending the liberties of Poland and that to some extent he succeeded. This is the exact reverse of the truth. Castlereagh wanted to renew the third partition of Poland; and he failed almost completely. 'Congress Poland' represented the victory of Alexander I and Czartoryski over Castlereagh and Metternich, the victory of Brougham over official British policy; or, in general terms, the victory of nationalism against the Balance of Power. It would be tempting to call this a Dissenting triumph, if the Dissenters had not made it so obvious that they had no clear idea what was at stake in the Polish question.

'Congress Poland' was the principal achievement of Vienna; and the Whigs had nothing to criticize in it except the few points at which Castlereagh had succeeded—Torun to Prussia, and Cracow as a Free City. Nor did they complain about the failure to unify Italy or Germany—the Sicilian constitution was their only care. The two great crimes in their eyes were the annexation of part of Saxony by Prussia and of Genoa by the Kingdom of Sardinia—the second of these at any rate soon condoned by Radical opinion. These two acts filled Whitbread with 'shame, remorse, and disgust'. He condemned 'forcing people to abandon their ancient govern-

ments'—a curious reversion to the Tory principle of legiti-
macy. If the Whigs put forward any general proposition, it
was that small states, however constituted, should not be
eaten up by large ones; and this consorted well enough with
the Radical belief that all foreign affairs were a corrupt conspiracy of the Great Powers.

Napoleon's return in the Hundred Days deluded the Whigs
into thinking that the age of Fox had come again. Like
Napoleon himself, they tried to revive their youth and to
stage a repeat performance. Grey moved against the war in
the Lords; first Whitbread, then more formally Lord George
Cavendish, in the Commons. Burdett, the Radical, said that
'if the principle of interfering in the concerns of a foreign
government was once acknowledged, wars would be eternal
—despotic governments would always be at war against free
states'; quite in the old vein. It all came to nothing. Napoleon was defeated at Waterloo and sent off to St. Helena—
there to receive tributes of books and admiration from Lady
Holland. Parliament did not debate the peace settlement until
February 1816. By then the European treaties were nearly a
year cold. There was hardly a comment on them. Whig
criticism turned only on the peace of Paris with France. Holland in the Lords, Romilly and Horner in the Commons,
attacked the implied guarantee to the Bourbons. Horner said
that the best guarantee of peace would be a free constitution
for France. Lord John Russell, with his habit already formed
of claiming the British constitution as a private property of
the House of Bedford, was glad that the principle of legiti-
macy had not prevailed a century ago: 'his own family in
that event must have stolen into obscurity, branded as
traitors, and stripped of all the honours with which the Crown
had laden them.'[1] The strongest Whig complaint was against
the British army of occupation in France. They should perhaps have defeated France; deprived her, if necessary, of
territory; and should then have withdrawn into 'insulation',
relying only on the British fleet.

[1] *Hansard*, new series, xxxii, 34.

Events at home gradually stirred a root-and-branch condemnation of the Vienna settlement. Peterloo obliterated Waterloo, or rather established the belief that it had been fought for the same oppressive cause. Since the Tory government were practising repression at home, it followed that they were conducting a repressive policy abroad. The Concert of Europe became a conspiracy against popular liberties everywhere, an 'Amphyctonic Council' designed to conduct 'auctions of subjects'.[1] This belief was consolidated by the revolutions in Naples and in Spain. Whigs and Radicals alike condemned the Concert and wanted to defend liberty by war. The Whigs spoke also of the Balance of Power in Europe—a Balance in which England should be on the side of liberal countries against the despots. Radicals repudiated the phrase, but the conflict of principle did not seem to matter when all alike arrived at the same practical conclusion. Holland, usually pacific, said over Naples: 'Deeply rooted as was his abhorrence of war, he would never say that the state of the country, or the embarrassment of our finances, was a reason for abstaining from it when it was necessary for the honour of the nation.'[2] Brougham said over Spain: 'In the better times of England, a menace, certain to be supported by war, would have stopped hostility and secured peace.'[3] He was by no means the last who wanted to combine 'a menace, certain to be supported by war' with a reduction in military and naval expenditure.

The friends of the old order sought to preserve it by remaining at peace. The Radicals talked of war for 'the liberties of Europe'—using the phrase in a sense very different from Pitt's. Radicals bemoaned the Spanish constitution; applauded the independence of the Spanish colonies. Radicals —Hume, Bowring—set up the Greek Committee; floated the Greek loan, to their subsequent discredit; tried to buy ships for a Greek navy on the quiet. Greece was the first of many enthusiasms for 'a people struggling rightly to be free', an

[1] Lord John Russell, *Letter to Lord Holland* (1819).
[2] *Hansard*, third series, iv, 1062. [3] *Hansard*, third series, viii, 1434.

enthusiasm in which classical learning and national principle, commercial interest and unselfish idealism, were strangely blended. The Radicals had a limitless confidence in British power, though they despised and distrusted those who exercised it. They preached simultaneously isolation and universal interference, wishing to stand aloof from all Continental entanglements and yet to defend liberty against all the world.

Cobbett is an extreme example, the most fervent and opinionated of Radicals. He regarded all foreign policy as a fraud by the old order, THE THING; and he rejoiced that the debt left by the Napoleonic wars made any active policy impossible. He even accused his fellow Radicals of supporting the Greek cause solely for the profit they hoped to make out of the loan. Yet he wished to brandish British naval power in the face of the world and particularly against Russia and the United States—enemies singled out largely because other Radicals regarded them with some favour. Twenty years after his death, a pamphlet assembled his writings on foreign affairs under the title, 'Cobbett's Reasons for War against Russia in defence of Turkey'. He denounced the Tsar as the Autocrat; and the worst of Russia's crimes was clearly not any interference with the liberties of others, but her challenge to British supremacy at sea. Here are two quotations. Cobbett wrote in 1822:

Ministers *ought* to send as many ships as they can muster, to carry a message to the Autocrat, requesting him, in very civil language, to march his Cossacks back from the confines of the dominion of the Turk, and, in case of non-compliance, to take, burn, sink, or destroy, or batter down all that they possibly could belonging to the Autocrat.

In 1829, after Navarino, he flattered himself on his foresight. His remarks have every quality of popular Radicalism —the naval boasting, the contempt for other countries, the criticism of the ruling classes:

I saw, and I said that I saw, the most imminent danger to our *dominion*, not over beggarly colonies in the North of America, not over blacks and sugar Islands, not over our '*Empire of the*

East'; but great and imminent danger to our all in all; namely to our dominion of the seas, given us apparently by God and nature, enjoyed for nearly a thousand years; and next to the laws framed by our forefathers, that great source of all our greatness and all our renown. Talk of *'philanthropy'*; talk of *'universal liberty'*; talk of 'civil and religious liberty *all over the world'*; it is my business, and the business of every Englishman, to take care of England, and England alone. . . . It is not our business to run about the world to look after people to set free; it is our business to look after ourselves and to take care of our Country and Sovereign; and, if we descend to particulars, it is our first duty to take care that England shall have the dominion of the seas.

Why not put a stop to the growth of this giant? Because we have not yet paid for the *'victories'* which we purchased so dearly some years ago, and about which we made such a boasting and a bragging.

Here is an extreme version of the Dissent in foreign affairs which men expected would triumph with the passing of the Great Reform Bill—and of which some selected items did in fact triumph in the following thirty years.

II

DISSENTING RIVALS

URQUHART AND COBDEN

HISTORICAL reputations go up and down just like the length of women's skirts. We used to think that the Great Reform Bill marked the triumph of the capitalistic middle class, launched parliamentary democracy, and so on. Now we are told that it changed nothing in British politics. I suppose that is right so far as the composition of the House of Commons goes. The electors still thought mainly of local considerations. The members came from the same class as before and acted from the same motives—family connexions or trading interests, private ambitions or idealistic quirks. All very true, very instructive; but those who regard it as decisive fall into the error of imagining that the House of Commons is the sum of its parts. They suppose that if we describe every member of parliament, then we shall have described the House of that day. The same outlook underlies the *History of Parliament*, on which some of my most admired colleagues are working. When I heard of the project, I couldn't help reflecting that a History of Parliament existed already, at least for more modern times. We call it *Hansard*, or—more grandly—*Parliamentary Debates*. No doubt the accumulated biographies of members will be of much interest to the social historian—and perhaps even explain some intrigues for office. But the history of parliament is to be found in what members heard and said, in what they felt, not in what they were.

Like other collective bodies, the House of Commons has its own rules of behaviour. Its character may change even though its individual members remain the same. The 'bought'

40

House of 1841 emerged from the most corrupt of all general elections; yet it rose five years later to a height of unselfish wisdom when it repealed the Corn Laws. Or consider the House elected in 1935 with a large majority behind Baldwin. Who could have supposed that it would sustain Winston Churchill through the greatest of our wars? The members of parliament after the Reform Bill were no doubt exactly what they had been before. Yet the House, and with it the whole political world, was entirely different. Only after the general election of 1906 was there something of the same atmosphere: the feeling that the old order had perished, a new day dawned —the feeling which Hilaire Belloc recorded so well:

> The accursed power which stands on Privilege
> (And goes with Women, and Champagne, and Bridge)
> Broke—and Democracy resumed her reign;

The last line I will here omit.

It was not so much the Reform Bill in itself, nor even that a Whig government was in power after forty years of supposed exclusion. It was rather the triumph of public opinion. Nowadays governments do everything; and in retrospect we think of the Reform Bill as having been carried by the Whig government. That is not how it appeared at the time. Contemporaries thought of the Bill as having been carried by the reforming majority in the House of Commons, with some assistance from ministers. The reformers were confident that what they had done for the electoral system they could do for everything else—for slavery, the East India Company, the Established Church, Poor Law, local government, and of course foreign affairs. They were right. This was a new age. These were the great days of the private member. Patronage was declining steadily—not so much because of Reform as from the same causes as produced Reform. Modern party organization had hardly begun. The member of parliament could follow his own bent, act according to his own judgment. Every government between 1835 and 1874 fell because of defeat in an existing House of Commons, not because of defeat at the polls; striking evidence of what we now call derogatorily 'the French system'.[1]

The independent members of the eighteenth century had been distinguished by their silence, though even this had sometimes determined the fate of governments. Now the private members became talkative. They initiated debates, laid down the law on policy, demanded information. The two greatest debates on foreign affairs in this period—the Don Pacifico debate in 1850, and the motion for an inquiry into the Crimean war in 1855—were both initiated by an independent Radical, Roebuck. Blue books swelled in number and size, particularly—a revealing point—blue books laid by command of the House. Questions were asked of ministers for the first time, the system becoming regularized in the eighteen-forties. Mr. A. C. Turner has distinguished seven pertinaceous questioners on foreign affairs in the twenty odd years before the Crimean war: Hume, Cutler Fergusson, Dudley Stuart, Urquhart, Roebuck, Anstey, Layard.[2] Urquhart and Layard had some firsthand knowledge of foreign affairs. The others were enthusiasts for a nation or a cause. Four of the seven were Scots, a feature repeated later. Perhaps Scots ask more questions. Or, more likely, the Scots, as a small nation, sympathized more easily with the national claims of others. The Welsh had a similar sympathy with the Boers at the end of the century. And of course the Irish who began to appear in parliament after Catholic emancipation always responded in this way—except in one case. The Irish, being Roman Catholics, were the only Radicals who never backed the unification of Italy. In the eighteen-thirties Italy was not yet a live issue. What was then important was that Catholic emancipation brought powerful reinforcement to the cause of Poland.

This was not of course the only reason why Poland became

[1] Disraeli's government of 1874–80 was the first to survive to the next general election with its majority undimmed.

[2] A. C. Turner, *The House of Commons and Foreign Policy, 1830–1867*, thesis in Bodleian Library.

the symbol of Radical foreign policy. The Polish revolt happened just at the right time, exactly when the Radicals were looking for some question in foreign affairs to be enthusiastic about. Poland enabled them both to denounce the 'Holy Alliance' and to demonstrate their solidarity with the Radicals in France. Nor did they need to decide between treaty rights and the national principle. They could demand the restoration of the constitution in Congress Poland, promised in the treaty of Vienna; and yet at the same time, like the Poles themselves, claim the frontiers of 1772. None of the Radicals thought of going to war. They believed that public opinion would be as irresistible internationally as it had been at home. Hume, as enthusiastic for Poland as for public economy, said in April 1832: 'he was decidedly convinced that the expression of a strong opinion by the Powers of Europe would preclude the necessity of going to war.'[1] O'Connell developed the same theme:

The effect of the Reform Bill would be, to give the democratic principle in this country an impulse it had not yet received, and that spirit, urged on by the sympathy the people had for liberty, would press upon the Government of this country—would press, too, upon the stock-jobbing government of France—and would compel the unpopular monarch there to sympathise with the feelings of the people of France, and encourage the people of Germany . . . to range themselves with every rational government; and insist upon justice being done to Poland.[2]

In the same debate Hume described the Tsar as 'a monster in human form'; and Sheil, the Irish member, said that 'he would not call him miscreant because the word was too poor and incommensurate with his depravity'.

The Polish cause was preached widely outside the House of Commons. The enthusiasm for Greece had come mainly, I think, from the upper classes; it demanded a classical education. Poland was the first enthusiasm of 'the democracy', though there was a literary element in it also. The most active centre was called the Literary Association of the

[1] *Hansard*, third series, xii, 661.
[2] 28 June 1832. *Hansard*, third series, xiii, 1137.

Friends of Poland; its organizer the poet Thomas Campbell, who hymned Kosciusko's fall forty years previously. It had branches in the principal Radical centres—Birmingham, Manchester, Glasgow—and also (a speciality of all anti-Russian agitations) in the seaports connected with the Baltic trade, Hull and Newcastle. This was a curious contradiction of the Cobdenite rule that we love our customers. Mass meetings had become the fashion during the Reform agitation. Now demagogues welcomed an alternative theme. Alternative, but not distinct. Reform and Poland were tied together. The liberation of Poland would lead to the triumph of Radical Reform, just as, the other way round, the partitions of Poland had touched off the wars against the French Revolution. An article in the *Westminster Review* carried this argument to the point of parody:

The people of England were the parties really made war upon, from the first junction of English ministers with the Holy Allies in 1792 to the termination in 1815. . . . If the Russians are driven over the Niemen, we shall have the Ballot; if they cross the Dnieper, we shall be rid of the Corn Laws; and if the Poles can get Smolensko[1] we too in our taxes shall get back to the ground of 1686. . . . Poland has its liberation to win, and so have we. We have both of us fallen among thieves; and we cannot do better than carry on the contest in concert.[2]

And what came of it all? Nothing much for Poland. Parliament voted the Polish exiles £10,000, a grant renewed annually until 1852. The price of a quiet conscience has gone up in the last hundred years like the price of everything else. It cost the men of Munich five million pounds to make themselves easy over the betrayal of Czechoslovakia. Though nothing was done for Poland, feeling simmered beneath the surface. In 1835 it was strong enough to prevent the appointment of Londonderry as Ambassador to St. Petersburg because of 'his want of sympathy with the known feelings of Englishmen in favour of the oppressed liberties and trampled

[1] Lost by Poland in 1686.
[2] *Westminster Review*, January 1831, quoted in J. H. Gleason, *The Genesis of Russophobia in England*, p. 132.

rights of Poland'. The Literary Association survived until the eighteen-eighties, when it was still supporting Poles who had gone into exile after the revolt of 1863. The Polish exiles educated the Radicals in Continental politics, and, incidentally, paid a penalty for doing so. Poles who associated with the Chartists were struck off the lists of the Treasury grant by Dudley Stuart. What the Radicals learnt from the Poles was hostility to Russia. The original target of Radical abuse after 1815 had been Austria, with Metternich as chief villain. Tories, not Radicals, were then suspicious of Russia. Now the Polish affair made Russia the mainspring of 'the Holy Alliance'. The switch of hostility was never complete. Austria became the chief bugbear of Radicalism whenever the Italian question blew up; and Poland had long periods of obscurity. But it is broadly true that after 1831 English Radicals regarded Russia as 'the gendarme of Europe'.

And something more. By a simple extension of reasoning, hostility towards Russia turned the Radicals into friends of Turkey. This certainly seems strange. How could the decaying Ottoman empire become a Radical cause, particularly for those who had backed Greek independence in the eighteen-twenties? Ingenious speculators have tried to find an explanation in the fact that Turkey had low, Russia high tariffs—an argument which Palmerston used when he presented Turkey as an enlightened progressive country. It is disturbing for this theory that Richard Cobden, the greatest Free Trader, was always anti-Turkish and pro-Russian. In any case it needed something more to supply the emotional atmosphere which henceforth clouded Anglo-Russian relations; and Poland did it. There had been no interest in Turkey during the war of Greek independence; and little talk even of British interests in the Mediterranean, except in the high Tory circle round Wellington. At the next crisis in 1833, when the Sultan was threatened by his rebellious vassal Mehemet Ali, Radicals argued that Great Britain should support Turkey as a barrier against Russia; and soon they were eager to support Turkey for her own sake.

The leading advocate of this new outlook was David Urquhart, the strangest Dissenter of the nineteenth century. Urquhart was no Radical by origin. Others started with general Radical principles and extended them to foreign affairs. Urquhart devised a foreign policy of his own and then found, to his surprise and irritation, that only Radicals supported it. As a young man he had fought for the Greeks. After the war he became almost a Turk by adoption. He introduced Turkish baths into England and preached them as a panacea against every physical and moral ill. He regarded Turkey as the ideal community—a view which Karl Marx took over when he held that Turkey was the one country which might pass into Socialism without experiencing capitalism. Urquhart had a winning way with him—a mixture of enthusiasm and charm. He captivated William IV and, with the king's backing, was made First Secretary at Constantinople. There he tried singlehanded to provoke a war between Great Britain and Russia. Instead Palmerston recalled him; and he retaliated by a lifelong vendetta, based on the absurd theory that Palmerston was in Russian pay.

Like E. D. Morel later, whom he much resembled, Urquhart was a man with an obsession. Or rather with two obsessions. He had first the obsession against Palmerston. All Radicals regarded foreign policy as a conspiracy of the governing classes. Urquhart put this in more concrete terms. Palmerston was a conspirator; his motive, Russian gold. Urquhart's more general obsession was against Russia. After the Polish revolt Radicals regarded her as a tyrannical power. Urquhart saw in her personified Evil; and, by a wonderful double stroke, condemned her not only as the centre of the Holy Alliance, but also as the paymaster of the revolution. He even claimed to have extracted from Mazzini the confession that the Italian revolutionaries acted under Russian orders. Like most enthusiasts—like Morel again—he was convinced that he was uniquely right and everyone else hopelessly wrong. His special discovery (hitherto known only to the Turks) was the Moral Law: the law which condemned all wars, but especially Russian wars against Turkey. He some-how managed to combine wild exaggeration of Russia's strength with a belief that the Ottoman empire could easily defeat her encroachments so long as it was not hampered by Western projects of reform. Here is a random sample of his obsession:

Russia chooses her own time; she prepares the events, she has them all under her own control. She sees on all sides at once. . . . She will be perfectly certain of success before she makes the move; and there is no reason whatever for her making the move before she is certain. Match with her knowledge, decision, secrecy, rapidity, and proximity our ignorance, uncertainty, changeableness, absence of disposable force, and distance, and then say if Russia has anything to apprehend from the awakened interests or aroused indignation of England.[1]

And so to the proof that Russia will be one day in Constantinople, the next day in Persia, and the week after pouring 50,000 men into India.

Urquhart appealed to respectable opinion without effect. He received a warmer welcome from the Chartists, and tried to persuade them that an enlightened foreign policy, and not universal suffrage, was the cure for all ills—presumably because taxes could be abolished after the destruction of Russia. His obsessions were strong meat precisely suited to the appetite of working-class Radicals, as cranky and self-instructed as himself. At Preston, for instance, his enthusiastic audience consisted of twenty Secularists and one Swedenborgian. He launched the Association for the Study of National and Interternational Affairs (subtitled, Committees for the Investigation of Diplomatic Documents)—the first forerunner of the U.D.C.; and earnest working men struggled through the blue books, scoring passages which proved the guilt of Lord Palmerston. For Urquhart taught not only that all diplomacy was wicked; he was also convinced that this wickedness could be detected from the records made by the diplomatists themselves. Later Dissenters have all accepted this doctrine, however much they reject Urquhart's line in other ways.

[1] Urquhart, *England and Russia*, p. vii.

The Eastern crisis of 1839 and 1840 put wind into Urquhart's sails. British support for Turkey was evidence that his writings had had their effect. But in other ways it was all wrong. Urquhart had preached support of Turkey against Russia, perhaps with the co-operation of France. Palmerston was working with Russia to defeat France—thus strengthening Urquhart's obsession that he was a Russian agent. Urquhart and the saner Radicals were drawn together. He objected to working with Russia, they to working against France. At Manchester Urquhart and Cobden actually appeared on the same platform. Members of Urquhart's Association went to Paris with assurances of British friendship. He himself visited Thiers, the French prime minister. The visit was not a success. Thiers 'received coldly my statement regarding the ignorance of Public Men in France'; and, 'when I observed him next he was sound asleep!' It is not necessary to go as far as Urquhart and the Radicals to find critics of Palmerston's policy in 1840. The difficulty is rather to find its supporters. *The Times* was strongly against it— always a good sign for a policy. The Cabinet was divided. Holland tried to repeat his uncle's stand against war with France; Clarendon, like most professional diplomatists, disliked a policy that was simple, resolute, and effective. The two addressed a formal minute of dissent to the queen—the last time, to the best of my knowledge, that this was done. Observe, I have got in a bit of constitutional history after all. The rest of the Cabinet were too feeble even to oppose Palmerston. He got his way by Bounce; perhaps also because the most difficult moments occurred when parliament was not sitting—an advantage which later Foreign Secretaries were usually denied.

The crisis of 1840 destroyed the 'liberal alliance' with France. Cobden described it later as 'the great diplomatic rupture . . . the effects of which have descended in increased armaments to the present time'.[1] Peel's Conservative government paraded its friendship with Russia; and in reply denun-

[1] Cobden, *Political Writings*, ii, 545.

ciations of Russia became a stock part of the Chartist programme. Lovett, the moderate Chartist, organized a demonstration of protest when the tsar came to London in 1844.
Harney, the extremist, presented himself against Palmerston
at Tiverton in the general election of 1847, though he repudiated Urquhart's charges of financial corruption. Harney's
candidature was an empty gesture. Urquhart however was
returned for Stafford. Himself an ineffective speaker, he persuaded Anstey to launch an impeachment against Palmerston
early in 1848 on twelve gigantic counts. Query—the last time
that an impeachment was moved in the House of Commons?
These activities, though futile, gave Palmerston a good deal
of trouble. He spoke on the hustings against Harney for over
two hours; and, in answer to Anstey and Urquhart, delivered
to a thin House the speech which ended with the famous
phrase that England has no eternal allies and no eternal
enemies; only her interests are eternal.

The campaign against Palmerston had chosen the wrong
target. In the weak Whig government of 1846–52, Palmerston
played skilfully for popularity; and he knew that this could
be gained by appealing to Radical sentiment. Not that he
needed much encouragement or inducement. He believed that
constitutional were better than despotic governments; and he
enjoyed lecturing foreign rulers. During the European revolutions of 1848 and 1849, he managed to create the impression that he was more favourable to them than his colleagues,
certainly more favourable to them than the Court or other
members of his class. English enthusiasm for foreign liberty
mounted steadily. In 1841 Sheffield was the only town in
England which celebrated the tenth anniversary of the Polish
rising. Even in 1846 only the Fraternal Democrats—a
Chartist offshoot—protested against the Austrian annexation of Cracow. But in 1847 W. J. Linton, a middle-class
republican, founded the Peoples' International League in co-
operation with Mazzini on a more respectable basis; and
Italy, unlike Poland, became a middle-class cause. Mazzini's
Roman republic—being directed against the Pope—won the

D

support of Tory Protestants as well as of Radical believers in liberty. Hungary united nearly everybody—opponents of Russia as well as of Austria, Chartists and middle-class Radicals. Universal applause from Palmerston to Harney greeted the workmen of Barclay's brewery when they mobbed the Austrian general Haynau—the hyena of Brescia —in the autumn of 1850.

Yet just at the moment when Palmerston seemed to have won Radical backing, there arose a rival Radical policy, which was ultimately to defeat him. It is called simply and justly Cobdenism. Richard Cobden was the most original and profound of Radical Dissenters; the one who most clearly passed from opposition to the formulation of an alternative foreign policy. The earlier Dissenters—and many later— were distinguished by generous emotion. They had limitless faith in British righteousness, especially their own, and wished—in the traditional Whig phrase—to promote 'civil and religious liberty all over the world'. Cobden was sane. Others relied on rhetoric; he reasoned. He was in fact the most powerful reasoner who has ever applied himself to practical politics; and the special characteristic of all his followers was 'to remain sane in a world gone mad'. When others grew more passionate, he became cooler. Again and again, men had to say of Cobden what Peel said: 'You must answer him; I cannot.'

Curiously enough Cobden was first drawn into thinking about foreign affairs by Urquhart. His two early pamphlets 'by a Manchester business man'—England, Ireland and America (1835) and Russia (1836)—were provoked by Urquhart's campaign in favour of Turkey. He laid his finger at once on the exaggeration in Urquhart's argument:

> Constantinople is about three thousand miles distant from Calcutta; are our Indian possessions of such value to the British people that we must guard them with operations so extended and so costly as would be necessary if the shores of the Bosphorus are to be made the outpost for our armies of the Ganges?[1]

[1] Political Writings, i, 20.

Cobden had been to Russia; and he believed that Russia, un-like Turkey, was capable of becoming a modern state. A Russian conquest of the Ottoman empire would be an ines-timable benefit for everybody. 'Not merely Great Britain, but the entire civilized world, will have reason to congratu-late itself, the moment when that territory again falls under the sceptre of any European power whatever.'[1] He described the advantages which Constantinople would gain from Rus-sian rule—noble public buildings, learned societies, the end of slavery, polygamy, and plague—and concluded:

To assert that *we*, a commercial and manufacturing people, have an interest in retaining the fairest regions of Europe in barbarism and ignorance—that *we* are benefited because poverty, slavery, polygamy, and the plague abound in Turkey—is a fallacy too gross even for refutation.[2]

Cobden refused to admit that any country, even Russia, was engaged in a calculated policy of world-conquest. The Balance of Power was 'not a fallacy, a mistake, an imposture, it is an undescribed, indescribable nothing; mere words, conveying to the mind not ideas, but sounds like those equally barren syllables which our ancestors put together for the purpose of puzzling themselves about words, in the shape of *Prester John* or the *philosopher's stone*.'[3] He never proposed to rely solely on the good will of other countries. In 1862, when advocating a naval agreement with France, he had 'no chimerical notion . . . of lowering your fleet to the level of the French fleet'.[4] Even Bright, who was sometimes nearer to pacifism,[5] did not plead 'that this country should remain without adequate and scientific means of defence'.[6] What Cobden urged was that existing naval armaments were enough to ward off any sudden attack and that, if danger

---

[1] *Political Writings*, i, 27.   [2] *Political Writings*, i, 142.
[3] *Political Writings*, i, 199.   [4] *Hansard*, third series, clxi, 61.
[5] By 'pacificism' I mean the advocacy of a peaceful policy; by 'paci-fism' (a word invented only in the twentieth century) the doctrine of non-resistance. The latter is the negation of policy, not an alternative, and therefore irrelevant to my theme. Hence my disregard for the Peace Societies.   [6] Speech on Foreign Policy at Birmingham, 1858.

threatened, our superior industrial resources would enable us to arm faster and more effectively than any potential aggressor.

More romantic Radicals would have agreed with this. They too rejected the Balance of Power; they too relied on British naval supremacy and believed that alliances were un-necessary. But what, they asked, about the sacred cause of universal liberty? What about freeing the oppressed peoples of the world? Cobden—it was his most challenging and origi-nal contribution—gave two answers. First, he denied Great Britain's moral superiority. He wrote of Poland:

> If it were the province of Great Britain to administer justice to all the peoples of the earth . . . then should we be called upon in this case to rescue the weak from the hands of their spoilers. But do we possess these favoured endowments? Are we armed with the powers of Omnipotence? . . . Do we find ourselves to possess the virtue and the wisdom essential to the possession of supreme power; or, on the other hand, have we not at our side, in the wrongs of a portion of our own people, a proof that we can justly lay claim to neither?[1]

Cobden had no difficulty in answering his own question:

> There is no country where so much is required to be done before the mass of the people become what it is pretended they are, what they ought to be, and what I trust they will yet be, as in England. . . . It is to this spirit of interference with other countries, the wars to which it has led, and the subsequent diversion of men's minds from home grievances, that we must attribute the unsatisfactory state of the mass of our people.[2]

Wars, in Cobden's view, did not occur by accident. They were an inevitable consequence of the undemocratic nature of British society. The armed forces were maintained princi-pally to provide jobs for the sons of the nobility. The aristo-cracy itself was 'essentially warlike'. It was 'a comforting delusion' that we were a peace-loving nation:

> We have been the most combative and aggressive community that has existed since the days of the Roman dominion. . . . It is

[1] *Political Writings*, i, 7.   [2] *Political Writings*, ii, 375.

displayed in our fondness for erecting monuments to warriors, even at the doors of our marts of commerce; in the frequent memorials of our battles, in the names of bridges, streets, and omnibuses; but above all in the display which public opinion tolerates in our metropolitan cathedral, whose walls are decorated with bas-reliefs of battle scenes, of storming of towns, and charges of bayonets, where horses and riders, ships, cannon and musketry, realize by turns, in a Christian temple, the fierce struggle of the siege and the battle-field. Mr. Layard has brought us very similar works of art from Nineveh, but he has not informed us that they were found in Christian churches.[1]

Cobden did not foresee the day when an Archbishop would bless the hydrogen-bomb.

In the second place, Cobden did not repudiate all interest in the liberties of other countries, some of which—unlike other Radicals—he knew at first hand. In 1849 he favoured keeping Russia out of Hungary by financial sanctions or, as he called it, 'stopping her supplies'. And he held that this policy had succeeded later in the year. What made Russia drop her demand on Turkey for the surrender of the Hungarian refugees, he believed, 'was the universal outburst of public opinion and public indignation in Western Europe'—an outburst that would have awkward practical consequences for Russia. At the end of his life he confessed: 'We all have our pet projects for interference abroad'—his was the liberation of Venetia. But the only way we could deter others was 'by setting a good example ourselves'. The key sentence of Cobdenism is to be found in his speech during the Don Pacifico debate in 1850—words which deserve to be printed in letters of gold:

The progress of freedom depends more upon the maintenance of peace, the spread of commerce, and the diffusion of education, than upon the labours of cabinets and foreign offices.

Hence the practical conclusion: 'as little intercourse as possible between Governments; as much connexion as possible between the nations of the world.' Cobden's favourite toast

[1] *Political Writings*, ii, 377.

was *no foreign politics*. 'Happy would it have been for us, and
well for our posterity, had such a feeling predominated in
this country fifty years ago!'—or a hundred years afterwards.
Before you dismiss Cobden as impractical, limited, or out of
date, reflect on this: aren't we all committed to the doctrine
that industrialization and material prosperity are the cures
for Communism, superstition, polygamy, and every other ill?
Cobden remains the voice of sanity in a world run mad.

In 1836 Cobden's opinions were those of an unknown
'Manchester business man'. By 1846 he had become one of
the most influential politicians in England. A few years later
his principles seemed to have been accepted as the basis of
British policy. This is often regarded as the triumph of
middle-class Liberalism, or more precisely of the Lancashire
cotton-trade, the Cottonocracy. This seems to me a crude
analysis. Cobden himself did not accept it. He pointed con-
vincingly to Bright's defeat at Manchester in 1857, after
opposing the Crimean war. No newspaper was more violent
against Bright and Cobden during that war than the *Manchester Guardian*, then more truly than now the voice of
Manchester capitalism. Who were the Cobdenites? I would
answer: not the business men, but the business-like, a matter
of mentality, not of class. Sociologists have very curious ideas
about the classes whom they claim to analyse, particularly
curious ideas about capitalists. I often wonder whether they
know any. Marx, for instance, drew a picture of the capitalist, ruthless, cold, always obeying the dictates of economic
law. But Engels, the one capitalist he knew, wasn't a bit like
that. Engels was vain, showy, emotional, generous. He
hunted twice a week with the Cheshire; was a member of the
Manchester Gentlemen's Glee Club; and loved a factory girl,
Mary Burns, who became his mistress. The capitalist does
not grow rich by being orderly, rational, modest; he does it
by flair, by backing a hunch. Keynes said: 'All business is a
bet'; and the successful business man is the unstable eccentric in an otherwise humdrum community. Was Hudson sane?
Was Rhodes? Was Northcliffe? Cobdenism may have repre-

sented the economic interest of the Lancashire cotton-trade considered in the abstract. But the mill-owners and merchants did not consider their interests in the abstract. Though mill-owners and merchants, they were also outstanding men in a Romantic age—heavily whiskered, living in the Gothic fan-tasies of Victoria Park, grandiloquent of phrase, patrons of Chopin and Liszt, readers of Tennyson, gambling in cotton futures. Why should such men follow Cobden's argument, let alone accept it?

Cobden's argument was in fact accepted by those who were accustomed to accepting arguments—a category usually found above and below the capitalist class. On the one hand were the high-minded members of the governing class who had thrown over 'influence' and thought only of public ser-vice—Peel and his associates, the sort of men who later staffed the Treasury in the age of competitive examination. It was their conversion, for example, and not the return of capitalist Liberal members of parliament, which carried Free Trade in 1846. Peel and the Peelites became the strictest adherents of Cobden, though none of them had a direct con-nexion with industry and few came to merit the name of Radical. Similarly the Cobdenites of the early twentieth cen-tury were not captains of industry. They were such men as J. A. Hobson and the Cambridge rationalists, detached intel-lectuals, some of them—Bertrand Russell, for example—of high social origin.

At the other end of the social scale, the working man in politics was more rational and less emotional than the capita-list, once he had got beyond the first instinctive revulsion of Chartism. The worker is by nature less imaginative, more level-headed than the capitalist. This is what prevents his becoming one. He is content with small gains. Trade Union officials think about the petty cash; the employer speculates in millions. You can see the difference in their representative institutions. There is no scheme too wild, no rumour too absurd, to be without repercussions on the Stock Exchange. The public house is the home of common sense.

It is a mistake to suppose that Cobden relied on materialistic arguments, as Palmerston for instance asserted that if an enemy landed on these shores Cobden and Bright would make a calculation as to whether it would be cheaper to take him in or keep him out. Cobden certainly used the argument that war was expensive; and so it is. But the appeal to economics was part of the stock-in-trade of the time. Palmerston claimed to be promoting the interests of British trade. Even Kossuth appealed to commercial advantage when he preached a crusade against Russia in 1851. Essentially Cobden appealed to reason, not to material advantage. What is more, he claimed to show that the most rational course was also the most moral. Free Trade and international peace were for him sacred ideals, beneficial to the whole human race, not to the dividends of a few.

I have of course made the conflict between Urquhart and Cobden, between the Romantic and the rational Radicals more explicit and conscious than it was in reality. The argument was worked out over a period of years. In 1846 say, after the repeal of the Corn Laws, all Radicals agreed that the governing classes were making a fine mess of foreign policy. All, or nearly all, applauded Palmerston's policy in 1848, somewhat to their embarrassment—some because he favoured the European revolutions, others because he did not intervene on their behalf. But the difference was growing; and it was openly shown in the great debate over the affair of Don Pacifico in June 1850—perhaps the greatest debate on the principles of foreign policy in our parliamentary records. For, apart from Palmerston's own triumph of vindication, the debate was dominated by Radicals on both sides. The traditional themes of foreign policy—the Balance of Power, the security of India, naval supremacy—were ignored. Discussion centred, as Radicals thought it should, on morality: how best do we promote the principles of peace and freedom in which we all believe?

The motion in favour of Palmerston was made by Roebuck —one of the few parliamentary Radicals who had worked, however distantly, with the Chartists, and the man who brought down the Coalition government in 1855 by his Radical demand for an inquiry into the conduct of the Crimean war. Back-bench Radicals gave Palmerston his majority at the end of the debate. But all the great names except Russell, who could hardly do other than defend his own Foreign Secretary, were on the other side—Molesworth, Graham, Peel, Gladstone, Cobden. All used Cobden's argument that non-interference was the best example; all acknowledged his leadership. I should perhaps except Gladstone. He made a preliminary mish-mash of the contradictions which he later elevated into a system. His zest for financial economy inclined him towards Cobden; his moral fervour tempted him to universal interference. At one moment he slipped back to old Toryism. 'Are we or are we not to go abroad and make occasions for the propagation even of political opinions which we consider to be sacred? I say we are not. . . . I object to the propagandism even of moderate reform.' At another he looked forward to the doctrines of Midlothian: 'The equality of the weak with the strong; the principles of brotherhood among nations, and of their sacred independence.' And in one passage he anticipated his belief in the Concert of Europe and the law of nations which, as he later claimed, divided him from Cobden and the Manchester School. It should be the duty of the Foreign Secretary 'studiously to observe, and to exalt in honour among mankind, that great code of principles which is termed the law of nations'.[1] Here *in embryo* was the case for his occupation of Egypt in 1882.

The majority which Palmerston won at the end of the debate was more in the nature of a caution not to do it again than a triumphant acquittal. His political stock was falling; and he left the Foreign Office—for ever as it turned out—at the end of 1851. The Great Exhibition seemed to mark the victory of Cobden's outlook. An intelligent foreign observer would have surmised in 1851 that British policy was set firmly on a pacific course. Yet in little over two years Great

[1] *Hansard*, third series, cxii, 543–90.

Britain was launched on a great war with the backing of public opinion, particularly Radical opinion. What beat Cobden? Most of all, the delayed swell of indignation against Russian tyranny. The old memory of Poland; the more recent memory of Hungary. In 1854 Joseph Hume did not move a reduction of the military estimates for the first time in his life; and Hume had been one of the Literary Friends of Poland in 1831. This swing of opinion received powerful reinforcement when Kossuth came to England in 1851. No foreigner except Garibaldi has had such a reception in England; none except perhaps President Wilson has exercised such a decisive influence on British policy.

Kossuth was entertained by the Corporation of Southampton and by the City of London. He was greeted by 100,000 people at Copenhagen Fields; by 200,000 in Manchester; and at Birmingham, where the calculations of the reporters gave out, by 'the entire population'. In true Radical fashion he appealed from the government to public opinion:

The basis of diplomacy is secrecy; and there is the triumph of absolutism and the misfortune of a free people. I hope soon this will cease, and foreign affairs will be conducted by that power which must be the only ruling one in a constitutional Government —public opinion.[1]

And in the very words of Urquhart: 'What is the principle of all evil in Europe? The encroaching spirit of Russia.' Only the remedy was slightly changed. Hungary, not Turkey, was the essential barrier against Russian aggression. 'It is Russian interference in the affairs of Hungary which put the bond of serfdom on the neck of Europe. . . . Without an independent Hungary there is no bulwark against Russian preponderance on the continent of Europe. . . . The freedom and independence of Hungary are indispensable to the independence of Europe against Russian encroachment and preponderance.'[2] Like those who took a similar line a century later, Kossuth denied that his policy would lead to war:

[1] *Kossuth; his Speeches in England*, p. 26.
[2] *Kossuth; his Speeches in England*, pp. 35, 43.

Should the Czar once more threaten oppressed humanity, violate
the sovereign rights of nations and their independence, take any
pretence whatever to put his foot on the neck of whatever people,
and drown Europe's liberty in blood, humanity expects that Britannia will shake her mighty trident and shout a mighty Stop. Be
sure this single word spoken with resolution to be good, as your
word will suffice, for this single word will neither cost you blood
nor money, spoken in time will save the life of myriads, avert
much bloodshed, and give liberty to the world.[1]

Maybe Kossuth was right. The Crimean war was not caused
by shouting a mighty Stop—a policy favoured by Palmerston
as well as by Kossuth. It was caused by failing to shout anything.

Yet once started the war seemed a Radical triumph. Here
was the challenge to the Autocrat, the Tyrant, which the
Radicals had preached ever since the Reform Bill. The Polish
exiles offered, though in vain, to form a Foreign Legion.
Mazzini, another exile, expressed the Radical hopes. This
was 'a War to solve once for all the problem of ages whether
man is to be a passive slave trampled on by brutal organized
force, or a free agent'. Harney the Chartist, now a working
journalist at Newcastle-on-Tyne, defined the war in two sentences: 'policy, alliance with the oppressed nations; object,
the annihilation of Russian supremacy.'[2] Urquhart reap-
peared; and on a new wave of popularity set up no less than
sixty-eight Foreign Affairs Committees—the strongest of
them at Hull and Newcastle—'to counteract the evils of
secret diplomacy'.

Yet Urquhart, with true Radical perversity, opposed the
Crimean war. He held that it was bound to be a hoax, 'absurd
and immoral', so long as it was run by the old gang, especially Palmerston. Indeed he was convinced that the war was
actually being run for Russia's benefit (the only rational
explanation certainly of the way the war was conducted).
Thus he wrote of the expedition to Sebastopol:

[1] *Kossuth; his Speeches in England*, p. 53.
[2] There is an excellent thesis on Harney by A. Schoyen in the Library
of London University.

Why select that port? Why not blockade the Russian ports and so destroy her trade? Why do you select a strong fortress, from which no hostile expedition ever sailed? And why do you leave unassailed the emporium of Odessa, which has always been the base of her operations?[1]

and so on. Urquhart's remedy was what a later generation called 'open diplomacy': policy ought to be discussed in the Privy Council, 'assembled in the constitutional manner by the Queen'—a Radical proposal despite its antiquarian fancy-dress. Harney carried the Foreign Affairs Committees against Urquhart in 1855. The Newcastle committee incidentally survived to support Disraeli during the next Eastern crisis in 1876—as did Harney himself from the United States in a pamphlet called *The Anti-Turkish Crusade*. Urquhart abandoned the British working class and, though never converted to Rome, henceforth looked to the Pope as his only reliable ally against Russia. But events justified his doubts. The Crimean war did not 'restore Poland and other oppressed nations'. Roebuck's motion for an inquiry into the conduct of the war was meant to inaugurate a Radical revolution. It brought down the Coalition government; put Palmerston into power. It did no more. Napoleon III, himself something of a Radical in foreign affairs, said truly: 'What should have been a great political revolution was reduced to a simple tournament.' It was the same at home. The Boer war, the first World war, the second World war, all led to a new order in politics. The Crimean war did not even produce a reform of the military system. Kossuth, Harney, and Roebuck seemed to have been wrong. The opponents of the war were justified by the event. Cobden and Bright triumphed, much to their surprise.

For their opposition, though noble and consistent, was ineffective while the war was on. Cobden indeed thought that all opposition to war was futile. He wrote in 1862 words which Morley often repeated during the first World war:

I was so convinced of the utter uselessness of raising one's voice

[1] G. Robinson, *David Urquhart*, p. 124.

in opposition to war when it has once begun, that I made up my mind that so long as I was in political life, should a war again break out between England and a great Power, I would never open my mouth upon the subject from the time the first gun was fired until the peace was made.

Bright too despaired of achieving any practical result—unlike Fox during the war against revolutionary France he never divided the House. He spoke to clear his conscience. 'For myself, I do not trouble myself whether my conduct in Parliament is popular or not. I care only that it shall be wise and just.'[1] And again, in his great peroration of 22 December 1854:

I am not, nor did I ever pretend to be, a statesman; and that character is so tainted and so equivocal in our day, that I am not sure that a pure and honourable ambition would aspire to it. I have not enjoyed for thirty years . . . the honours and emoluments of office. I have not set my sails to every passing breeze. . . . Let it not be said that I am alone in my condemnation of this war, and of this incapable and guilty Administration. And, even if I were alone, if mine were a solitary voice, raised amid the din of arms and the clamours of a venal press, I should have the consolation I have to-night—and which I trust will be mine to the last moment of my existence—the priceless consolation that no word of mine has tended to promote the squandering of my country's treasure or the spilling of one single drop of my country's blood.

Noble words. Yet there was danger in them. Bright wanted 'the priceless consolation' that his conduct should be 'wise and just'; he was less urgent to change the policy that he condemned. There was in Bright as in those who followed his example later, a high-minded passing-by on the other side. This was shown most clearly towards the end of his life when he resigned office in protest against the bombardment of Alexandria; and then did nothing to oppose its consequences.

Bright did not criticize the Crimean war as a pacifist. He challenged the advocates of war on their own ground, showing from the blue books that the war was unnecessary and that a wiser diplomacy could have avoided it. His arguments

[1] Speech of 31 March 1854.

triumphed with posterity, despite their failure at the time. More generally, he echoed Cobden in repudiating the Balance of Power. 'The whole notion is a mischievous delusion which has come down to us from past times; we ought to drive it from our minds.' He repudiated too the idea that we should fight for the liberties of others. 'It is not my duty to make this country the knight-errant of the human race':

What a notion a man must have of the duties of the . . . people living in these islands if he thinks . . . that the sacred treasure of the bravery, resolution, and unfaltering courage of the people of England is to be squandered in a contest . . . for the preservation of the independence of Germany, and of the integrity, civilization, and something else of all Europe![1]

Bright's speeches against the Crimean war were perhaps the greatest ever delivered in a parliamentary assembly. A hundred years afterwards they still throb with life. But they gave an unfortunate twist to the Radicalism of 'the Manchester School'. 'Non-interference' was for Cobden the beginning of policy. Bright often gave the impression that for him it was the end. He was content to stress 'as little intercourse as possible between Governments'. Cobden wanted to get on to the next stage: 'as much connexion as possible between the nations of the world.' No one has believed more strongly than Cobden in international co-operation, though not through governments. Yet thanks to Bright 'isolationism' became the hallmark of the Manchester School.

Public opinion was not swayed by these high arguments. It was merely disillusioned by the muddle and failure of war. To put it crudely, bad medical services at Scutari made Bright and Cobden the masters of British foreign policy. They remained unpopular during the war, and even after it. Bright was denied a hearing in Manchester (though his critics were also); and he was jostled in Market Street. In 1856 his health broke under the strain. He and Cobden both lost their seats at the general election of 1857. Yet soon they were on the top of the wave. The speech on foreign policy which Bright made

[1] Speech of 7 June 1855.

on his first visit to Birmingham in October 1858 was the speech of a victor, gay, confident, inspiring. He carried his audience with him as he demonstrated that for the last century and a half British foreign policy had been a waste of time and money except for 'the territorial aristocracy':

The more you examine this matter the more you will come to the conclusion which I have arrived at, that this foreign policy, this regard for 'the liberties of Europe', this care at one time for 'the Protestant interest', this excessive love for the 'balance of power' is neither more nor less than a gigantic system of outdoor relief for the aristocracy of Great Britain. (Great laughter.)

The applause was not simply because Birmingham was more enlightened than Manchester. Times had changed. Everyone now believed that foreign policy was a farce, a delusion.

In 1859 there was war again on the continent of Europe, and more clearly than the Crimean war a war of liberation: the war in which France and Sardinia drove the Austrians from Lombardy. But there was no agitation in England to take part, only to stay out. Kossuth made another tour, speaking in London, Manchester, Bradford, and Glasgow. His sole theme was non-interference. Since the isolationists had won, they could afford to be generous; and they conceded that they might support war under circumstances that were never likely to occur, much as the pacifists of the nineteen-twenties applauded the sanctions of the League of Nations Covenant so long as these remained theoretical. For instance, Bright said during the rather sham alarm which followed the French annexation of Savoy:

I am here as the representative of a great English constituency, who have no kind of business with this question except in so far as it affects the honour and interest of England. . . . All nations should say, England is a Power regarding her own interests mainly, not interfering in Europe when it can be avoided, and, when interfering, doing so, not for the sake of degrading one Power and exalting another, but in favour of those great principles of justice and moderation which are necessary to the transactions of great Powers if the peace of Enrope is to be preserved.[1]

[1] *Hansard*, third series, clvii, 1260–6.

This, strictly interpreted, was nearer to Gladstone's Midlothian speeches than to non-intervention.

There was still argument over foreign policy. Indeed debates on it increased steadily, reaching the unprecedented figure of 22 per cent of *Hansard's* columns in 1864.[1] But Palmerston and Russell, the two noble lords of the Crimean war, were now on the defensive, perpetually explaining that they had done nothing despite all their exertions. Dissent flourished even within the cabinet. Gladstone as prime minister once laid it down that the cabinet always accepted the advice of prime minister and foreign secretary when the two agreed. This was by no means his practice in the eighteen-sixties. More remote authorities played their part. The prince consort directed the cabinet Dissenters. Granville, a reluctant *homo regius* and the last of them, informed the prince of the moves made by Palmerston and Russell at one meeting; and the prince organized the opposition to these moves at the next. The prize for dissent can however be claimed, as so often, by a Russell—Lord John, now an earl and Foreign Secretary. Robert Morier, a rising British diplomatist and one of the few who knew something of Germany, persuaded Russell to abandon the rigid insistence that Sleswig-Holstein must remain under Denmark and instead to advocate partition on the national line. But when Russell tried out this policy, the cabinet 'pooh-poohed it'. He then instructed Morier to write a pamphlet on the *Dano-German Conflict*, criticizing the policy of his own government.[2]

Cobden was the real Foreign Secretary of the early eighteen-sixties. He negotiated the Commercial treaty with

[1] A. C. Turner, *The House of Commons and Foreign Policy*, thesis (Bodleian).

[2] This act did Morier much harm in his official career. Russell had swung back to supporting Denmark by the time the pamphlet was published; and Morier seemed to have behaved disloyally. Unwilling to embarrass his chief, he remained silent until 1870, when the Sleswig affair was over and Russell no longer in office. By then his reputation for disloyalty was firmly established in the Foreign Office; and nothing could ever shake it. There is no catching up with mud once it has been thrown. Hence: 'never deny; never explain.'

France; preached international arbitration; and was the first
to propose an agreed limitation of armaments. This is what
he meant by *No foreign politics!* He could not believe in his
own success. He wrote his longest and most carefully argued
pamphlet, *The Three Panics*, against the anti-French alarms
of 1860–1. The labour was unnecessary. The alarm was without reality, an echo of the past like the talk about French
hegemony during the occupation of the Ruhr in 1923. There
was more passion and energy in the agitation against intervention which Bright conducted during the American civil
war. This alarm too was exaggerated; but it had results of
profound importance in the political situation at home. It
brought the industrial working class over to the Manchester
School. Previously the workers, or at any rate their leaders,
had hankered after the emotional Radicalism of Harney and
Urquhart; they had been ready to applaud even Palmerston's
jeers against 'the honourable and reverend gentleman'. Now
Bright, stumping the country, was more concerned to defend
the cause of the North than to preach non-intervention; and
this did the trick. For the United States was then the symbol
of advanced democracy, whatever it may be now.

There is a striking illustration of the changed outlook.
When Poland revolted in 1863, a few Trade Union leaders
joined the various revolutionary exiles in meetings of protest;
but the most strenuous English protesters were 'intellectuals' of the Positivist School. Bright, on the other hand,
could count his working-class audiences by the thousand; and
every outstanding Trade Unionist sat on his platform. He
was no doubt still a mill-owner, still preaching the capitalist
cause of Free Trade. Nevertheless the English working man
of the day was following Bright, not Marx; admiration for
the United States had eclipsed regrets for Poland.

Conclusive triumph came to Cobden with the Sleswig affair
in 1864. There could hardly be a better case for British intervention: accessible to sea power; the freedom of the Baltic
at stake; British honour undoubtedly pledged. All to no
avail; and though Palmerston pleaded technical excuses—no

E

Continental ally, British forces locked away in Canada—it is difficult to believe, after reading the debates in the House of Commons, that the British government could have gone to war in 1864 under any circumstances. Nor was the negative decision one for the moment only. It remained unchallenged for more than forty years. Between 1864 and 1906 no British government seriously contemplated armed intervention on the continent of Europe.

At the Cabinet of 25 June, which finally resolved to do nothing, Russell, game to the last, sat scribbling formulas which might leave some loophole for action and counting his possible supporters, always a minority however often he counted. Palmerston 'held his head down . . . and then looking up said in a neutral voice, "I think the cabinet is against war" '.[1] Gladstone called this 'a tolerable, not the best, conclusion'—a tantalizing remark. What would the best have been? Some action? or more words? Cobden dominated the subsequent debate in the House of Commons. He put forward a series of negatives. 'We gain nothing by diplomatic meddling'; we should discard the idea of maintaining the Balance of Power; we have not the material strength to protect the weak against the strong. 'There is a right and a wrong in every case, and if we are always to choose one side or the other because it is thought to be the right, how is it possible we can ever enjoy any peace or quietness in this country?' He made one positive assertion: the House of Commons, not the Foreign Office, must determine foreign policy.[2]

When Palmerston replied, he sheered off foreign affairs and saved himself by surveying the Liberal record of his government—much of it accomplished against his will. Lady Palmerston listened to the debate in the Ladies' Gallery. When it ended at three o'clock in the morning Palmerston ran up the stairs to the gallery and embraced her. He triumphed over old age, but not over the Radicals.

[1] Morley, *Life of Gladstone*, ii, 117.
[2] *Hansard*, third series, clxxvi, 827–66.

III

GLADSTONIAN FOREIGN POLICY

THE CONTRADICTIONS OF MORALITY

BRITISH policy, or the lack of it, in the Sleswig affair marked the triumph of Cobdenism. 'No foreign politics!' became the rule. I feared that the following thirty years might leave me stuck for a subject and that I should have to retreat to the Positivists. They are worth a mention for their own sake. They were not profound thinkers; they had virtually no influence on their own time. But they anticipated in an uncanny way the ideas and outlook of some seventy years later. It is as though they had got on to the wrong wavelength and became audible only when Time turned the knob. In 1866 the leading Positivists brought out *International Policy*, so far as I know the first composite volume in which a number of writers laid down an ideal foreign policy.

Their starting-point was the Religion of Humanity, as developed by Western civilization. Western Europe was 'the recognized instrument of humanity' (Congreve). 'The vanguard of the human family is to be found in the Western section of Europe alone' (Harrison). You will recognize the contemporary ring. What they wanted in practice was 'a full programme of general policy' between England and France. The Anglo-French union would be, by definition, idealistic and unselfish. It would make war 'only as an act of police'—that pregnant metaphor. England would withdraw from India and renounce her rights in China; Gibraltar and Malta would become 'international police-stations' (Beesley).

Who else should be included in this human family? The small states of Western Europe of course—they always come in as an afterthought. Not the United States. Alliance with them would be 'national egoism'. Russia should be excluded. She was 'extra-European and semi-Oriental' (Harrison); 'alien to the movement of later European thought. . . . She should follow, assimilate, not attempt to lead' (Congreve). The Positivists were much troubled about Germany. Was she civilized at all? Sometimes they thought of accepting western Germany and handing the rest over to Russia; sometimes they said that Russia should take charge as far as the Rhine. The Franco-Prussian war removed their doubts. The Positivists were the only group in England to demand active intervention on the side of France—particularly at a meeting in St. James's Hall on 10 January 1871. Thenceforth they were anti-German as well as anti-Russian. Frederic Harrison, the most active of them, survived to advocate universal military service before 1914 and to hail the first World war as the triumph of Positivism.

This is little more than a frivolous intellectual aside. If it had rested with the Positivists, there would have been no effective Dissent in the last forty years of the nineteenth century. We must thank Gladstone for having something to talk about. The champion of Dissent and also its ruin. In 1864 he was the leading opponent of Palmerston in the Cabinet; in 1870 he was the only member of the Cabinet to advocate intervention, if only moral, in the Franco-Prussian war. In 1876 he whipped up Dissenting fervour over foreign policy to a point never reached before; in 1882 he launched Great Britain on the course of Imperialism by occupying Egypt. Gladstone's contradictions puzzled himself. He was a Dissenter who was always explaining away his dissent, though still more his agreement; a Radical who preferred the company of aristocrats; an enemy of Power who loved to wield it. There was an explanation though he never found it. He was one of a rare type: the demagogue-statesman. I use neither word in a pejorative sense. Statesmen, alas! we have always with us; and demagogues were by no means new. Wilkes, Orator Hunt, Feargus O'Connor, were recognizably akin. Bright belonged with them, despite his loftier tone and his acceptance of office under Gladstone. Essentially he wanted to sway opinion, not to direct affairs. Gladstone combined the two characters. He was Sir Robert Peel and Feargus O'Connor rolled into one—an explosive combination. He was undoubtedly a statesman of the highest order, for instance as administrator and financier. But he also became a great popular orator, perhaps, though his speeches do not keep their freshness, the greatest there has ever been. Gladstone the demagogue would launch a great campaign with mass applause. Then Gladstone the statesman would intervene and would insist that the campaign had no purpose unless he were returned to power. This has been called, somewhat charitably, 'his sense of right timing'. Others have found harder words for it.

Gladstone was, or became, the People's William. He knew perfectly well that only the people were wholeheartedly on his side during the great stir over the Eastern question. Yet he was always emphasizing the few aristocrats who were with him; and his Midlothian speeches suggest that he thought it more important to have the Earl of Rosebery on the platform than two thousand people in the hall. He wrote to Mme Novikov in November 1876:

I am sorrowfully of opinion that, though virtue of splendid quality dwells in high regions with individuals, it is chiefly to be found on a large scale with the masses; and the history of Courts is one of the most immoral parts of human history.[1]

Again in May 1877:

I am acting in the Eastern question against the Government, the Clubs, the London Press (in majority), the majority of both Houses, and five-sixths or nine-tenths of the Plutocracy of the country. These make up a great Power. Against them, is, I believe, the true nation.[2]

Observe the reserves, the meticulous accuracy with which he calculates the righteous few. On the public platform his exceptions were even more pronounced:

[1] W. T. Stead, *The M.P. for Russia*, i, 269.
[2] W. T. Stead, *The M.P. for Russia*, i, 356.

We cannot make our appeal to the aristocracy, excepting that which must never be forgotten, the distinguished and enlightened minority of that body of able energetic, patriotic, liberal-minded men, whose feelings are one with those of the people. We cannot reckon upon the clergy of the Established Church . . . , subject again and always in each case to those most noble exceptions. . . . Above all these, and behind all these, there is something greater than these—there is the nation itself.[1]

After a great oration to tradesmen and farmers, he would step into a carriage and drive off to the mansion of the Duke of Sutherland or the Duke of Westminster. This is a parable of his political career.

The favour of the Cobdenite Radicals had carried Gladstone to leadership of the Liberal party. His dislike of increased expenditure on armaments—indeed on anything— gave him a bond of sympathy with them. But whereas they were rational and modestly reluctant to interfere with others, he was emotional and convinced of his own peculiar inspiration. He was by nature an interferer, by training a man of Power. It seemed to him perfectly natural that the Cobdenites should put him in office to carry out a policy the reverse of theirs, just as he expected Radicals to vote for him so that he could appoint Whig ministers—and was angry when Chamberlain queried the arrangement. He had a particularly maddening trick of pretending not to understand why he was being criticized. Thus he once asked Palmerston 'in all good humour' not to identify him with Cobden and Bright; and added, 'I do not know their opinion with any precision.' A surprising ignorance. Cobdenite principles are among the few political doctrines that a child can understand, as no doubt many children did in the eighteen-sixties. Yet Gladstone, with his inexhaustibly subtle intellect, found them beyond him. This, if true, was a poor tribute to the education he had received. He repudiated the Manchester School more elaborately in one of his Midlothian speeches:

What is called the Manchester School has never ruled the foreign policy of this country—never during a Conservative Government,

[1] Gladstone, *Political Speeches*, ii, 354.

and never especially during a Liberal Government. . . . It is not only a respectable, it is even a noble error. . . . But however deplorable wars may be, they are among the necessities of our condition; and there are times when justice, when faith, when the failure of mankind, require a man not to shrink from the responsibility of undertaking them.[1]

The essence of Gladstone's foreign policy was his belief in 'the public law of Europe'. This divided him from the Manchester School; and, though he never admitted—probably never appreciated—it, drew him perilously near to Urquhart. On this ground he supported the Crimean war, a support which he never repented. It was, he said, 'not an arbitrary combination, but a representation of the great European combination of Powers, acting against Russia, to vindicate and enforce against her the public law of Europe'.[2] Though the Crimean war failed of its purpose, he refused to draw the moral, as Bright and Cobden did, that the public law of Europe was a will-o'-the-wisp, an empty phrase. But he could never decide whether to draw the moral that, the rulers of Europe having proved untrue to the public law, the people should be invoked to enforce it, or whether the rulers of Europe would respond if the rulers of Great Britain preached it more emphatically. Or rather he drew both morals and pursued them simultaneously, to his own and everyone else's confusion.

The dilemma took some time to work itself out. In 1864 Gladstone seemed on the same side as Cobden when he opposed Palmerston's policy. In fact he would have worked with France to enforce 'the judicial principle' in the Sleswig question, but would do nothing alone—a very different attitude. Still it came to the same thing in practice. In 1869 Gladstone defined his position in words at first sight almost indistinguishable from those Bright had used in 1861. The queen had complained that England was ceasing to count in the world. Gladstone replied:

Is England so uplifted in strength above every other nation, that she can with prudence advertise herself as ready to undertake the

[1] *Political Speeches*, ii, 30.
[2] 8 June 1855. *Hansard*, third series, cxxxviii, 1071.

general redress of wrongs? . . . Is *any* Power at this time of day
warranted in assuming this general obligation? . . . It is dangerous
to assume an advanced position . . . promise too little rather than
too much . . . seek to deter the strong . . . seek to develop and
mature the action of a common, or public, or European opinion . . .
but beware of seeming to lay down the law of that opinion by her
own authority.[1]

Look at the words more closely. Bright advocated non-
intervention 'except in so far as it affects the honour and
interest of England'; and he would show in any particular
case that the exception had not arisen. Gladstone's exception
is public morality. Certainly England should not act alone;
but she should seek to act with others in the name of 'a
common or European opinion'. This was what he later
called 'the Concert of Europe'; and what was the Concert
but a new form of 'the Holy Alliance'—most detested of
names to a Radical? Press Bright's policy to its conclusion,
and you arrive at isolation, inaction except in case of actual
invasion. Press Gladstone's doctrine to its conclusion; and
you have universal interference, as the Radicals discovered
too late.

The cleavage between Gladstone and the Radicals was
almost revealed at the outbreak of the Franco-Prussian war.
The government negotiated new treaties to secure the neutrality of Belgium; and Gladstone justified them in a speech
packed with characteristic conjuring tricks. Unlike a true
Cobdenite, he used conventional arguments, but with a refine-
ment of taste, as much as to say: 'Others may like these,
though they do not appeal to me.' He began with the treaty
of 1839 which was 'an important factor and a weighty element in the case'. Then he referred to the Balance of Power,
'the force of which we must all feel most deeply'. After this
he switched to moral arguments. Belgium was a model of
ordered freedom. 'The day that witnessed its absorption
would hear the knell of public right and public law in Europe.'

[1] Gladstone to General Grey, 17 April 1869. Morley, *Life of Gladstone*,
ii, 316.

England could not stand quietly by 'and witness the perpetra-
tion of the direst crime that ever stained the pages of history,
and thus become participators in the sin'.[1] Ten years later,
speaking retrospectively, he had forgotten everything except
the moral issue:

If we had gone to war we should have gone to war for freedom,
we should have gone to war for public right, we should have gone
to war to save human happiness from being invaded by tyrannous
and lawless power.[1]

This argument would have applied to the defence of any small
country anywhere in the world. Would Gladstone in fact
have used it if Belgium had been at the other end of the
world? Was it not the Balance of Power and British security
that were really at stake? A few Radicals thought so. Jacob
Bright, John's brother, divided the House against the new
treaties. He received five votes, about the lowest point of
Radical dissent. Yet when it came to the practical consequence, Gladstone swung back to a Cobdenite attitude.
Cardwell, the Secretary of State for War, objected that Great
Britain did not possess the armed force with which to execute
the treaties. Gladstone replied: ' *When* it is seriously intended
to send troops to Antwerp or elsewhere abroad, immediate
measures must be taken to increase our forces.'[3] In other
words, as Cobden had argued and as Radicals were to argue
until well on in the twentieth century, England's geographic
position and industrial resources made it unnecessary for her
to maintain great armaments until war had broken out. Gladstone endorsed this argument; and his agreement so delighted
the Radicals that they overlooked his more profound diver-
gence of principle.

The Franco-Prussian war raised a further problem of Dissent for Gladstone, though for hardly anyone else except the
Positivists. When the Germans mooted the annexation of
Alsace and Lorraine without consulting the inhabitants, Gladstone wished to voice 'the reprobation of Europe'. 'Europe

[1] *Hansard*, third series, cciii, 1787.
[2] *Political Speeches*, ii, 32.   [3] Morley, *Life of Gladstone*, ii, 339.

is entitled to utter it, and can utter it to good effect.' He was not clear what form this reprobation should take—perhaps the Russian plan 'of not recognizing that in which we have had no part'. At any rate silence would be 'a standing reproach to England'.[1] The cabinet refused to follow Gladstone's lead. He then wrote an article in the *Edinburgh Review*, anonymous but signed in every line, advocating his policy and, by implication, criticizing his cabinet colleagues. He was much surprised when they discovered that he had written the article and still more so when they resented it. A prime minister attacking the policy of his own government in public is a curiosity even for dissent. Curious, but not unique. Indeed, on the principle that anything done twice becomes a tradition, it is now an accepted convention of the constitution. For Bonar Law did just the same. Writing as 'a Colonial', he denounced in the columns of *The Times* the settlement of war debts which his government had made with the United States.[2]

Now I come to a far bigger affair: the Bulgarian Horrors of 1876, which aroused the greatest storm over foreign policy in our history. Why did the Horrors have such a tremendous effect? The answer is simple: they were the political crime of the century. We find this difficult to understand. We live in a harder, more ruthless age. A million and a half Armenians massacred by the Turks in the first World war; five million Jews massacred by the Germans in the second; the atomic bombs dropped on Hiroshima and Nagasaki—these have hardened us into thinking the massacre of some twelve thousand Bulgarians a triviality. The later nineteenth century was a more civilized era. The stir of 1876 was moral first, and Dissenting by accident. It sprang neither from the intellectual Radicalism of Cobden, nor from the blustering John Bull Radicalism of Cobbett and Urquhart. It inherited rather the moral passion of the abolitionists against slavery, by no means a Dissenting affair. Many of the Radicals had

[1] Morley, *Life of Gladstone*, ii, 346–8.
[2] Evelyn Wrench, *Geoffrey Dawson and his Times*, p. 215.

opposed the maintenance of the naval patrols against the slave trade on grounds of economy. There was a symbolic link: the two thousand people who gathered in a tent to watch a magic-lantern shown of *Uncle Tom's Cabin*, and at the end passed a resolution demanding aid for the oppressed Bulgarians. It is revealing too that Lord Shaftesbury—a Tory but also a leading humanitarian—should have been deeply associated with the Bulgarian agitation. Where Cobden had preached non-intervention, the agitators of 1876 wished to invoke the Concert of Europe and were ready even to make an alliance with Russia. To put it crudely, they were not Radicals, but the high-minded; and so far as Radicals joined in, it was because they too were high-minded despite their political outlook.

The Radicals with the coolest heads kept aloof. Bright never liked the positive side of the agitation, though he was willing enough to attack Disraeli. The surviving Urquhartite committees at Hull and Newcastle-on-Tyne first supported Disraeli and then later wished to impeach him for betraying Turkey. Swinburne wrote a pamphlet called *Note of an English republican on the Muscovite crusade*. Hyndman, a Radical though not yet a Socialist, 'could not see that the desire to emancipate Christian populations . . . was sufficient justification for supporting the growing and aggressive despotism of Russia'.[1] This vision was belatedly conferred on him in 1914. There was an odd contrast with an emotional stir on a smaller scale which had blown up ten years earlier—the prosecution of Governor Eyre for harshness in suppressing an alleged rising in Jamaica. The intellectual supporters of Eyre—Carlyle, Froude, Tennyson, Ruskin—were now all indignant for the Bulgarians. The minority who organized the Jamaica committee against Eyre—Huxley and F. W. Newman—were unmoved by the Bulgarian Horrors. The Positivists remained firm against Russia, and still firmer against emotionalism in politics. Congreve and Frederic Harrison both attacked Gladstone in the *Fortnightly Review*,

[1] Hyndman, *Record of an Adventurous Life*, p. 180.

to the embarrassment of John Morley, the editor, who was
hoping to clamber into politics on the Gladstonian band-
wagon. George Potter, the working-man Positivist and
former member of the First International, was particularly
outspoken. He wrote in October 1876: 'Governments cannot be expected to carry out the dreams and desires of men
troubled with religious or philosophic fervours.'

The campaign over the Bulgarian Horrors was conducted
by men who had little previous experience of political action.
It was, I suppose, the only political campaign in which all
the leading historians of the day took part—certainly the
only one in which they all took part on the same side. Freeman, Lecky, Froude, Kinglake, Bryce, Seeley, Stubbs,
Carlyle, J. R. Green; not one was left out. It is often said,
though not by me, that historical studies promote a moderation and caution in political judgment. These great historians outdid any politician in the virulence of their utter-
ances. Freeman was naturally the wildest. He startled even
the St. James's Hall Convention by his cry:

Would you fight for the freedom of the Empire of Sodom?

And another sentence nearly lost him appointment to the
Regius chair a few years later:

Perish the interests of England, perish our dominion in India,
rather than that we should strike one blow or speak one word on
behalf of the wrong against the right.

But other historians did pretty well. J. R. Green wrote:

I am afraid we are drifting into war—into war on the side of the
devil and in the cause of Hell. . . . I love England dearly; but I
love her too well to wish her triumphant if she fight against human
right and human freedom.

Carlyle, with characteristic wrongheadedness, actually
favoured the Russians because they were tyrants: 'In our
own time they have done signal service to God and man in
drilling into order and peace anarchic populations all over
their side of the world. . . . They have a clearer hold of the
great truth that obedience to the rightful authority is a

sacred duty.' It was at this time, incidentally, that Carlyle coined the phrase—'the unspeakable Turk'.

What was there in the contemporary historical approach which made the leading historians of the day so fervent for morality, so enthusiastic for the Bulgarians, so eager to interfere? I am tempted to spend a whole lecture on an inquiry so fascinating. They were not usually friends of national freedom; most of them became Unionists a few years later. Nor were they Radical in ordinary politics. Their specialist interests ranged widely over epochs and areas. None except Freeman really knew anything about the Balkans, past or present. What they had in common, I think, apart from Carlyle was their belief in Progress. They were all secular missionaries, a role to which many historians still aspire. The outrages angered them by seeming to cast doubt on their faith. Again all, except J. R. Green, were men of Power, glorifying Empire and the rise of modern States. They were all, without exception, fervent patriots, eager to crush anyone who should challenge the moral code of their civilization. They were more concerned to batter the Turks than to liberate the Bulgarians.

These historians, for the most part, also managed to combine Progress and Christianity. Here is the second new element in the Bulgarian Horrors affair. While atheist Radicals stood aside, men usually Conservative were driven into temporary Dissent by their religious outlook. The Bulgarian Horrors provided the only occasion in our history when the majority of the leaders of the Established Church were against the government—the only occasion, at any rate, since the Glorious Revolution. When one considers the record of the Bench of Bishops—voting solid against the Reform Bill, supporting capital punishment for almost every conceivable offence from Romilly's day to ours, always finding excuses for the men in power—it gives a shock of surprise to find Bishops on the side of Dissent: Bishop Fraser of Manchester, the Bishops of Ely, Norwich, Exeter and Oxford. This unusual response was no accident, nor even a conversion to humanitarianism. A few Evangelicals came in from the old emotion which had made them abolitionists; but the High Churchmen predominated. In fact the agitation over the Bulgarian Horrors was in large part a bye-product of Ritualism. Liddon, the leading Puseyite, was the first Englishman to attack the Turk when he preached at St. Paul's on 13 July 1876. Pusey himself sent a letter of blessing to the Convention at St. James's Hall.

Liddon and his associates brought to politics the dogmatic passion which they had developed in their conflicts over 'churchmanship'. Liddon wrote on 15 January 1878: 'To me the cause of Russia in this struggle appears plainly to be the cause of Righteousness'; and on 18 April 1878: 'If I were a soldier or sailor in Her Majesty's service, I should feel obliged to retire, if I could, in the event of a war with Russia' —an outlook echoed at the Curragh in 1914. The Ritualists were not much concerned about the sufferings of the Bulgarians nor about their national liberation. Russia represented for them an abstract cause, as she was to do again for others in the twentieth century: in their case, the cause of the Orthodox Church. The liturgy of the Orthodox Church determined their political outlook. Liddon wrote to Stead:

I have always regretted any prominence which has been given to the Pan-Slavonic aspects of the Eastern question. That aspect does not interest other races, and it puts the matter on a *lower* level than that which it ought to occupy.[1]

In other words, it was a nuisance that the Bulgarians were human beings as well as Orthodox Christians. Since the Ritualists were pro-Russian, the Roman Catholics, led by Manning, stood aloof. They would not actually support the Turks as Urquhart had urged them to; they would have liked to back Austria-Hungary—the course they followed in 1917. This put the Irish Radicals in a difficulty. A few sympathized with a people struggling rightly to be free. Most of them evoked the old cause of Poland, and thus joined hands with the

[1] 22 October 1878. W. T. Stead, *The M.P. for Russia*, ii, 8.

Positivists at the other end of the scale. The Bulgarian Horrors produced strange bedfellows.

The agitation needed something more than Ritualists and historians if it were to have any practical effect. It needed an organizer, a driver. The first stir came from Lewis Farley, once a Turkish consul, now secretary of the League for the Protection of Turkish Christians—perhaps because he had lost money in Turkish loans. The movement really got going when it was taken up by W. T. Stead, at that time editor of the *Northern Echo* at Darlington—incidentally another town on the north-east coast. Stead always called himself a Radical, but he too was in his way a man of Power. He was the first popular journalist, the forerunner of Northcliffe and Horatio Bottomley. He did many things which were outside the normal Radical pattern. It was Stead who suggested sending Gordon to Khartum. In 1884 he started the Big Navy agitation. He ended as a spiritualist. Or, to be exact, he went down with the *Titanic*, which was symbolically appropriate. He was also an enthusiast for Russia; an enthusiasm which Alexander III repaid by confining his reading of the English Press to Stead's *Pall Mall Gazette*—or so he told Stead.

Stead claimed to have learnt from Cobden's writings that 'second only to healing the fatal schism between the two great English-speaking peoples, there was no political duty so obvious and imperious as that of removing the ill-feeling and jealousy which existed between Russia and England'.[1] He did not learn much else from Cobden, certainly not reason or self-control. In the Bulgarian affair Stead joined hands with Olga Novikov, a self-appointed Russian propagandist, who had come to England originally to promote the reunion of the Churches, and was turned into a Pan-Slav by the death of her brother when fighting as a volunteer in the Serbian Army. Mme Novikov was a gifted writer—according to Stead, her pamphlets were second only to the Midlothian speeches in promoting the Liberal victory of 1880. She also

[1] *The M.P. for Russia*, i, 380.

made full use of her personal charms. Stead writes of his 'relations of passion with her', whatever that may mean. Gladstone wrote affectionate letters to her, and used to take her arm at public meetings. Froude addressed her as 'my dear Miss'—a bad sign. The Russian Embassy disapproved of her. They preferred to import a couple of Bulgarians, who were trundled round the country much as the League of Nations Union imported an Abyssinian in 1935, I think from Paris.

It was Stead, too, who got hold of Gladstone and persuaded him to write his famous pamphlet on *The Bulgarian Horrors*. There was a link of temperament between them. Stead went to prison for his campaign against 'the maiden tribute of modern Babylon'; Gladstone was ready to ruin his career rather than give up reclaiming fallen women—a cause on which he spent all-told £83,000. Mr. Kingsley Martin told me that *The Sexual Life of the Victorians* would be a more rewarding subject than Dissent over Foreign Policy. I rejoice to have satisfied him, as I satisfied the constitutional historians in my last lecture. Gladstone was a powerful, but a dangerous, ally. He could never shake off the attitude of a statesman. He tried to evade this and to speak only as a private citizen. His first speech was to his constituents at Blackheath—a characteristic evasion; and when he went on tour, he operated from Longleat, the seat of the Conservative Marquis of Bath. But he always felt that the agitation was pointless unless the Conservative government was put out and a Liberal government put in. Yet this too was pointless, since the leaders of the future Liberal government, according to Gladstone's own account, would be Hartington and Granville, both of whom were indifferent to the Bulgarians.

Stead, Freeman and the rest were remote from these political calculations. They had no interest in substituting one set of politicians for another. In true Radical fashion, they wished to supersede the existing system and start afresh. This was shown by the Convention which they organized at

St. James's Hall. In name it recalled the Chartist Convention of 1839; in outlook it anticipated the Councils of Action of 1920. It was far more than a conference or a political demonstration; it was an anti-parliament, designed to represent the true spirit of England. Hence politicians were excluded: they were all part of THE THING. It was planned to have delegates elected from each town by a town-meeting, presided over by the Mayor. But the plan could not be worked in time. In a few places, elections of a sort were organized by the local Reform Club—an unfortunate intrusion of politics. Most of the delegates were self-appointed, as usually happens in Radical demonstrations. The speakers at the Convention—a two-day marathon of oratory—were clergymen, historians, novelists: Trollope, the Bishop of Oxford, Bryce, Liddon, Freeman. The presence of Sergeant Simon did not deter Freeman from referring to Disraeli as 'the Jew in his drunken insolence'—at this time anti-Semitism was still a Radical attitude. Gladstone was the only prominent politician who spoke, and he claimed to be in retirement. He spoke as a theologian and historian, as a moralist, as anything but a party representative. At the end he ostentatiously gave his arm to Mme Novikov.

The only practical outcome of the Convention was the founding of the Eastern Question Association, with William Morris as treasurer. It was his first experience of politics; and it had an unexpected result. He discovered that only the working class judged honestly and fearlessly in foreign affairs; and the discovery turned him into a Socialist. In the twentieth century this discovery was to be made afresh by innumerable Radical critics of official foreign policy; and it led them too on to the Morris road. Certainly the agitation proved disappointing after the St. James's Hall meeting. There was a significant pointer when *The Times* went over to the Turkish cause. Its motto has always been: 'Be strong upon the stronger side'; and naturally it switched when the movement flagged. The change took place in a characteristic way—to be repeated by Dawson in 1938. Delane the editor

F

read 'a strong pro-Russian article' in the paper while on holiday in Scotland. He hurried back and changed the policy of the paper overnight, hoping that no one would notice. The Proprietor however noticed. He concluded that Delane was losing his grip and sacked him within the year—a satisfactory outcome.

It is, I suppose, always easier for a Dissenting movement to hamper the government than to impose an alternative policy of its own; and the agitation over Bulgaria was no exception. In the autumn of 1876 it was strong enough to prevent Beaconsfield from actively supporting Turkey, supposing that he had ever seriously wished to do so. It could have enforced co-operation with Russia only if it had overthrown the government, as Gladstone recognized; and this was never a serious possibility. Beaconsfield had merely to sit tight and let the storm blow over. Moreover attention shifted in the early months of 1877 from the Bulgarian Horrors to the diplomatic manœuvrings at the Constantinople conference—less profitable material for a popular agitation. In April Russia went to war against Turkey; and thereafter the Turks were too busy defending Plevna to have any time for the further massacre of Bulgarians. The indignation worked itself to a standstill.

What is more, the Convention at St. James's Hall failed to eclipse Parliament as the sounding-board of the nation. On the contrary, the Convention was forgotten once Parliament reassembled. The historians and clergymen ceased to count. Gladstone had to take the lead, whether he would or no. In May 1877 he tabled five resolutions. Two condemned Turkey. Everyone, including Derby the foreign secretary, could agree with these. The other three called for intervention in co-operation with Russia and the Concert of Europe. These were the essence of Gladstone's policy, as of the Eastern Question Association's. Freeman wrote: 'If the fault of our Government leaves us no choice between the aggrandisement of Russia and the bondage of Bulgaria and other revolted lands, then we must choose the aggrandisement of

Russia.'[1] But when it came to the point Gladstone drew back. He declined to be seen in public with Mme Novikov. In the House he moved only the first two resolutions, though not formally withdrawing the others—a truly Gladstonian touch. Even so the breach with the Cobdenites was revealed during the debate. Jacob Bright opposed even the surviving resolutions. John Bright did not speak and gave this embarrassed explanation:

There are times when much might be said, when, notwithstanding, it may be wise to be silent. Whether I was wise to remain silent during the recent debate I must be allowed to be the most competent judge.[2]

Gladstone got almost the full strength of the Liberal party into the division lobby—223 against 354; but to no purpose. Stead doubted 'whether there were at any time more than sixty or seventy avowed coercionists in a House of 658'; but sixty or seventy votes for a coherent policy would have been better than 223 who did not know what they had voted for. Gladstone could never stop looking for a line 'very beneficial to the party'. He wrote to Granville on 23 May: 'I could wish that there were some other question of real magnitude likely to reunite them; but I do not see any.'

The tug-of-war was repeated again and again. The Radical coercionists wanted to capture Gladstone for their policy. He wanted to translate Radical enthusiasm into Liberal votes. Neither side succeeded. On 31 May Gladstone went to Birmingham to inaugurate the National Liberal Federation. Shortly before this Chamberlain wrote to Stead: 'The future programme of liberalism must come from below. It is evident we have no inspiration to expect from our present leaders.' Not that he thought much more highly of Gladstone, but 'he is the best card we have'. The card could however never be played to any effect. Gladstone delivered himself with passion, but his only practical statement was: 'We are rolling the stone of Sisyphus up hill, and the moment we

---

[1] *Daily News*, 24 October 1876.   [2] *Daily News*, 22 May 1877.

cease to push, the stone begins obstinately to roll down again.' In other words, as Stead observed, Beaconsfield and Gladstone cancelled each other out. The isolationists triumphed, though without understanding why. Great Britain did not join Russia in liberating the Bulgarians; nor did she go to war for the integrity of the Ottoman empire. As Bright remarked, she would much better have done nothing on high principle from the start.

The events in the early months of 1878—the sending of the fleet to Constantinople, the tension with Russia from February until May—are of less interest from our point of view than those of the previous year. There was no longer an alternative policy to Beaconsfield's; only resistance to it— and not much of that. Even Gladstone now spoke in purely negative terms, the Concert of Europe temporarily forgotten: 'My purpose has been, with extremely inadequate means, and in a very mean and poor degree, but still to the best of my power, for the last eighteen months, day and night, week by week, month by month, to counterwork as well as I could what I believe to be the purpose of Lord Beaconsfield.'[1] But Gladstone could not rouse himself for a campaign of simple non-intervention. He left it to Bright, Bradlaugh, and a few Radical Trade Unionists. They resumed the leadership of what movement there was; and this obscured the conflict between them and Gladstone in the previous year. As a matter of fact, Gladstone was hard put to it to find a high ground of moral Dissent when he came to the peace settlement. He denounced the Cyprus convention with Turkey as 'an insane covenant'—which indeed it was. But when he sought to define 'the question broader than any of the questions that have divided Tories from Liberals during the last half-century', he could only complain of secret diplomacy:

whether you are substantially to be governed, your future pledged and compromised, your engagements enormously extended, the necessity for your taxes enlarged and widened, not only without your assent, but without your knowledge, and not only without

[1] At Oxford, 30 January 1878.

your knowledge, but with the utmost care to conceal from you the facts.[1]

Yet Gladstone advocated much more than full parliamentary discussion of foreign affairs. He advocated, or claimed to advocate, an entirely new system of foreign policy. He attempted to display this system in his Midlothian speeches —speeches which retain a high reputation for oratory largely, I suspect, because they are never read and in which the twists of Gladstone's utterance make it almost impossible to pin down his thought. Much of his doctrine was still straight Cobdenism, despite his repudiation of the Manchester School:

Is it in the nature of things—is it in the design of Providence, that besides the concerns of the vast Empire over which this little island rules, we should be meddling in the business of almost every portion of the globe?[2]

Often there was rhetoric acceptable to every sort of Radical:

Fortresses may be levelled with the ground; treaties may be trodden under foot—the true barrier against despotism is in the human heart and in the human mind.[3]

His 'right principles of foreign policy' all came from the common Radical stock: economy, peace, no needless entanglements, equal rights of all nations, a love of freedom. All except one: the Concert of Europe. This, slipped in as No. 3, was the one on which Gladstone laid most stress. It was the one which opened the way to British leadership and British action on the highest moral grounds. He said at West Calder on 27 November 1879:

Strive to cultivate and maintain, ay, to the very uttermost, what is called the concert of Europe. . . . And why? Because by keeping all in union together you neutralize and fetter and bind up the selfish aims of each. . . . Common action means common objects; and the only objects for which you can unite together the Powers of Europe are objects connected with the common good of them all.[4]

[1] At Southwark Liberal Association, 20 July 1878.
[2] *Political Speeches*, i, 183.   [3] *Political Speeches*, ii, 219.
[4] *Political Speeches*, i, 115–16.

Again on 22 March 1880:

The high office of bringing Europe into concert, and keeping Europe in concert, is an office specially pointed out for your country to perform. . . . That happy condition, so long as we are believed to be disinterested in Europe, secures for us the noblest part that any Power was ever called upon to play . . . for it is the work of peace and the work of good will among men.[1]

Finally on 2 April:

I prefer the policy of the Government of Mr. Canning, and the policy of the Government of Lord Grey, and the greater part of what was done by Lord Palmerston in foreign affairs, and by Lord Russell in foreign affairs, to that which is now recommended to you.[2]

No doubt. But it was in opposing these policies, particularly the policies of Palmerston and Russell, that Cobdenism had triumphed.

The general election of 1880 was fought solely on foreign policy. It was certainly a decisive defeat for Beaconsfield. But, in the words of Alice, who had won? Gladstone used the moral indignation over the Bulgarian Horrors and the Radical belief in non-intervention to commit the electorate to leadership of the Concert of Europe. But he did not act even on his own principles. Once in power they had to be subordinated to parliamentary tactics. Wilfred Scawen Blunt, the friend of Egypt, tells a revealing story. He heard from Gladstone an inspiring defence of national independence. But when he said: 'May I send some message from you to the Egyptians?' Gladstone drew back and said: 'I think not. . . . Let them read what we say in Parliament.' Blunt adds this profound comment: 'His own personal impulses for good . . . were like his taste for music, his taste for china, his taste for bric-à-brac, feelings he would like to indulge, but was restrained from by a higher duty, that of securing a parliamentary majority.'[3] This was shown in his behaviour over

[1] *Political Speeches*, ii, 221–2   [2] *Political Speeches*, ii, 351.
[3] Blunt, *Secret History*, p. 238.

Cyprus. He had denounced its acquisition; he described it as
'a valueless encumbrance': he foretold the woes that would
follow and which have indeed followed. Left to himself, he
would have handed it over to Greece, who had every right to
it. But once in office, he merely repudiated the guarantee of
Asiatic Turkey which had been its price. To cede Cyprus
would lose votes; therefore it was impossible. Thanks to
Gladstone, we have Cyprus round our necks to this day.

Worse was to follow. The occupation of Egypt in 1882
marked Gladstone's decisive breach with Radicalism. Indeed
it ruined Radicalism for more than a generation. It began
modern British Imperialism; and Egypt was the pivot of
imperial policy for seventy years afterwards. Why on earth
did he do it? How did Gladstone, the advocate of economy
and peace, take a step which led inevitably to great armaments and imperial aggrandisement? Part of the answer is
accident, drift. He thought to bluff Egypt as he had bluffed
Turkey the year before. He hoped, as Bright did till the last
moment, that sending the British fleet to Alexandria would
be enough; it would not have to do anything. Instead his
bluff was called. There were more remote, more truly Gladstonian calculations. The troubles in Egypt flared up just
after Gladstone's failures in Ireland. Egypt paid the price for
the assassination of Lord Frederick Cavendish in Phoenix
Park; just as, in the reverse direction, Gladstone later championed Home Rule for Ireland in order to atone for his betrayal of national freedom in Egypt. The pattern was
repeated in 1893 when Ireland again benefited from
the prickings of Gladstone's conscience over Egypt and
Uganda.

His most shameless argument was a perverse 'continuity'.
He had criticized the original intervention in Egypt by the
Conservative government in 1879; he had foretold the
entanglement that would follow; therefore he was not to be
blamed for getting entangled. 'It would not have been in
keeping with the propriety of things to reverse the attitude
which we found occupied by the British Government in

Egypt.'[1] Yet he had fought a general election solely in order to reverse the attitude occupied by the British government not only in Egypt but all over the world. All that survived of Midlothian was a claim to be acting in the name of the Powers. This claim, and the display of financial rectitude, demoralized the Radicals and confused their opposition. Blunt, who almost staved off the occupation of Egypt single-handed, thought that 'the general feeling of the country was violent against all "lawlessness" '—in some muddled way Arabi was transformed into a Bashi Bazouk. Chamberlain, himself eager for action, was probably nearer the truth: 'The Egyptian intervention was unpopular with the majority of the Liberal party, and nothing but Mr. Gladstone's personal influence could have secured its permanence.' A curious sentence by the way—Gladstone repeatedly pledged himself against permanence. So, if Chamberlain is to be believed, Gladstone deceived himself as well as the Radicals.

Chamberlain adds: 'If Mr. Bright had led an agitation against it I believe he would have been able to destroy the Government.'[2] Bright hesitated to go against Gladstone much as he had kept silent in 1877—hence his remark the following year: 'I prefer to treat the Egyptian incident rather as a deplorable blunder than as a crime.' Still he resigned; and his speech on resignation gave a clear enough lead if anyone had wished to follow it:

For forty years at least I have endeavoured, from time to time, to teach my countrymen an opinion and doctrine which I hold,— namely that the moral law is intended not only for individual life, but for the life and practice of States in their dealings with one another. I think that in the present case there has been a manifest violation of International Law and of the moral law.[3]

Gladstone used his old weapon of defence against the Manchester School; he made out that he could not understand what Bright was driving at. He wrote to the queen: 'Mr.

[1] 12 February 1884. *Hansard*, third series, cclxxxiv, 703.
[2] Chamberlain, *Political Memoir*, p. 81.
[3] *Hansard*, third series, cclxxii, 723.

Gladstone is obliged to admit that he does not clearly comprehend Mr. Bright's present view.'[1] Others comprehended, but passed by on the other side. Sir Wilfred Lawson was virtually the only Radical to raise his voice against a policy that was 'unwise, impolitic, ignoble, and unjust'. The Quaker ironmaster Pease thought that the occupation would not benefit the Egyptians; therefore he would not vote for it. But he would also not vote against it. Even Labouchere, the pronounced Little Englander, had a short Jingo spell: 'Intervention was absolutely necessary if England was to remain the great Power she was . . . otherwise India would not be worth one year's purchase.' Bryce launched the theme that would sustain a thousand university lectures: 'he was bound to acknowledge that there was such a thing as continuity in foreign policy.' Only nineteen voted against the government; and ten of them were Irish.

Gladstone's frenzy of righteousness swelled as he plunged deeper into the Egyptian slough. He had church-bells rung, guns fired, on the news of the battle of Tel-el-Kebir; and he wrote to Mme Novikov:

We and the whole country are in a state of rejoicing, and I hope of thankfulness to Almighty God who has prospered us in what I feel and know to be an honest undertaking. . . . Whether the England of 1882 deserves to be regarded by some in Russia with a jealous eye, or whether we, too, have been labouring in the common interests of justice and civilization a little time will show. We certainly ought to be in good humour, for we are pleased with our Army, our Navy, our Admirals, our Generals, and our organization![2]

All this because some wretched Egyptian peasants had been butchered by Sir Garnet Wolseley. The Gladstonian enthusiasts trailed along behind. Stead was always strong for the occupation. Morley, who was just being jobbed into parliament by Dilke, swallowed it with his usual thin reluctance. Those who had remained cool in 1876 were now the only

[1] Gladstone to Victoria, 15 July 1882. *Letters of Queen Victoria*, second series, iii, 310.   [2] *The M.P. for Russia*, ii, 130.

opponents of intervention—along with the lone fighter Blunt. Frederic Harrison wrote an article called 'Money, Sir, Money!' which much embarrassed Morley. It was a land-mark as the first, rather crude attempt to expose the financial basis of Imperialism. Hyndman and his Social Democrats could now attack British policy without seeming to help Russia. Bradlaugh, backed by the Unitarians, made an odd contrast with the Ritualist parsons of St. James's Hall.

The critics of the Egyptian affair were convinced that it sprang from sordid financial motives. Protection of the bond-holders, the Rothschilds with the *whole* of their capital in Egyptian securities,[1] Money, Sir, Money—there was the key to the mystery. Labouchere took the same view when he sold out his Egyptian holdings to free himself from sin. Of course there was something in it. Still, the bondholders and the Rothschilds could never have got their way—if indeed this was the way they wanted—without the moral fervour com-mon to Gladstone, Stead, and Chamberlain. Old-fashioned Jingoism may have been Tory, though I doubt even that. Imperialism was a product of Radical enthusiasm. The Im-perialists were isolationists so far as Europe went. They wanted to ignore the Continent and to discharge the 'British mission' in the rest of the world. Every Imperialist believed that Great Britain had achieved the highest form of civiliza-tion ever known and that it was her duty to take this civiliza-tion to 'the lesser breeds without the law'. These were Radical beliefs. The coloured races should receive the emanci-pation which had been denied to the Bulgarians. Cromer, the leading figure in Egypt, was a Liberal. So was Milner, who first worked in Egypt and then became the chief maker of the Boer war. Whenever Milner returned to England, he spent his time with Liberals—Asquith, Haldane, Grey—never with Tories. Rosebery, the most Imperialist of Prime Ministers, had sat on the platform throughout the Mid-lothian speeches. And of course Chamberlain the greatest Imperialist of all, would have led the Liberal party if he had

[1] Blunt, *Secret History*, p. 343.

not fallen foul of Gladstone. The Imperialists had little respect for tradition. Kipling, the bard of Empire, was so contemptuous of the Establishment that he refused all decorations, including even the Order of Merit; and he described Edward VII as 'a corpulent voluptuary'. It was not surprising that the Radicals did not know which way to turn.

Egypt was decisive from the practical as well as from the moral point of view. It dictated the shape of British foreign policy for the next twenty years. It destroyed 'the liberal alliance' with France—a cause sacred to both Cobden and Urquhart. It forced Great Britain into association with the Triple Alliance, which was most distasteful to the Radicals. Yet the only alternative (short of withdrawing from Egypt) was to make the British Navy supreme against all comers. Stead first advocated this logically enough in 1884. Most Radicals gave a more embarrassed answer. Though in theory Big Navy men, they detested the expense involved and tried to make out that the British Navy could remain the best in the world without any increase in the estimates. Egypt reduced them to confusion again and again. Gladstone himself sent Gordon to Khartum and then refused to help him. A good many Radicals, including Morley, protested against the expedition to the Sudan in 1885. But when it came to a vote, only nineteen Radicals went into the lobby with Labouchere against it.[1] They could never decide whether they wanted to abandon Egypt itself. In 1886 Bradlaugh and sixty-two Liberals voted against the mission of Drummond Wolff, which might have produced an international agreement over Egypt; seventy-three Liberals voted in its favour. Labouchere spoke against the motion, but abstained from voting.

The Radicals plucked up courage whenever the Conservatives were in office, knowing that their Dissent would be ineffective. They ran away when it was a question of voting

---

[1] These and other figures are from R. Gross, *Factors and Variations in Liberal and Radical opinion on foreign policy 1885–1899* (thesis in Bodleian).

against a Liberal government; and soon started the legend
that they were being betrayed by their leaders, when in fact
they did not want their policy to succeed nor even knew what
policy they wanted. It was safer to fall back on Local Option
or Welsh Disestablishment. Even Keir Hardie never voted
in any division on foreign affairs during the parliament of
1892–5, so as not to squander I.L.P. energies in any field not
directly related to social reform.[1] Radical waverings were
clearly shown in the lobbies. Ninety-seven supported
Cremer's motion for immediate withdrawal from Egypt in
1887, when Salisbury was safely in office. Only thirty-four
voted against the annexation of Uganda by the Liberal
government in 1894, itself a consequence of the occupation
of Egypt. Joseph Arch and the rising young Radical Lloyd
George both voted in favour of annexation—partly out of
moral fervour against the slave trade (and against the Roman
Catholic missionaries who represented the rival French
Imperialism), partly from loyalty to Gladstone, who had
opposed it violently but unsuccessfully in secret. Or again on
armaments. One hundred and twenty voted against the Conservative Naval Defence Act of 1889. Only thirty-one voted
against the Liberal estimates of 1895—estimates not only far
greater than the Conservative ones, but greater than those of
the previous year which had driven Gladstone from public
life. It is not surprising under such circumstances that in the
general election of 1892 over half the Liberal addresses,
including those of Gladstone, Labouchere, Morley, and Grey,
failed to mention foreign affairs at all.

Gladstone had ruined the Radicals. Yet he alone could
raise a spark. His conscience never ceased to trouble him. He
knew that the occupation of Egypt was against 'the moral
law' whatever he might say to Bright; he believed that reconciliation with France was 'a righteous cause'. But he would
not do anything 'detrimental to the party'. Gordon at
Khartum was made to pay the penalty for Gladstone's sin in
Egypt. Gladstone discovered in the dervishes 'a people

[1] So he told Dilke. Gross, 310.

struggling rightly to be free', and in the Mahdi a national hero where Arabi had been none. But when the death of Gordon discredited the government, Gladstone swung round and restored his prestige by challenging Russia to war over the incident at Pendjeh. Stead, Chamberlain, and Mme Novikov were the only people in England to speak out on the Russian side, though even Dilke later admitted that the Russians had been entirely in the right. Out of office, Gladstone criticized Salisbury's reliance on the Triple Alliance, and denounced the Mediterranean Agreements as 'measures of a premature character which will tend to fetter the free discretion of this country'. Yet when he returned to power in 1892, he made only the most perfunctory inquiry about these agreements at the Foreign Office, and accepted a brazen denial of their existence. He implored Rosebery, imperialist and friend of Germany, to become foreign secretary; and he allowed Waddington, the French ambassador, to be more or less ordered out of the country for trying to settle the Egyptian question. Even when he did leave office rather than agree to the increased naval estimates, he kept his Dissent secret for the sake of the party—hoping no doubt that Rosebery and the other Imperialists would have him back again sooner or later. After all his doctor told him that he would live to a hundred.

He retained enough vitality at any rate to repeat the Bulgarian campaign over Armenia in 1895 and 1896. There was the same combination, or rather contradiction, of principles. There was genuine humanitarianism, reinforced by the Christianity of the martyred people. Once more Gladstone invoked a treaty to justify British interference. In 1876 it had been the peace of Paris; now it was the Cyprus convention—an invocation the more piquant in that Gladstone had once denounced the convention and had himself repudiated the guarantee to Turkey which was part of it. Again he sought to win votes for the Liberal party. The only practical effect was to drive Rosebery to resign its leadership. And again Gladstone extolled the Concert of Europe. Yet he knew that this

Concert was a myth; and his devoted supporter Canon MacColl declared: 'The Concert of Europe has been the parent of all the mischief in Armenia.'[1] Gladstone's last appearance was on 24 September 1896. He denounced Abdul the Damned, and then proposed: 'We should break off relations with the Sultan; if Europe threatened us with war it might be necessary to recede as France had done in 1840— without loss either of honour or power.'[2] A strange analogy, and a yet stranger policy. Bluffing to the last; hoping that Abdul Hamid would be taken in by an empty show. And if not? There would be no loss either of honour or power. We could always 'recede'. This was Gladstone's last testament in foreign affairs and one, I fear, accepted without demur by many of his later disciples. 'Let us obey the dictates of morality; if they land us in difficulties, we can "recede"'— at the expense of the Armenians or the Abyssinians.

[1] MacColl, *Memoirs and Correspondence*, p. 208.
[2] Morley, *Life of Gladstone*, iii, 522.

IV

THE NEW RADICALISM BEFORE 1914

WHEN we leave Gladstone gesticulating on the platform of St. George's Hall and move into the twentieth century, it is a new act, almost a new play. There was Dissent in plenty, more coherent, more persistent, more profound. Yet it was less effective, at any rate in the short run. On the one hand the Radical Press was more powerful and better informed. The nineteenth century had nothing to show like the galaxy of the *Manchester Guardian*, the *Nation*, the *Economist*—to say nothing of the Socialist papers. For the first time there were Dissenting writers of literary distinction: J. A. Hobson, Norman Angell, H. N. Brailsford, Lowes Dickinson. Not greater perhaps than Cobden, but more prolific and read by more people. Yet the Radicals in parliament carried less weight so far as foreign affairs went. They were admirable, but rather trivial: Sir Wilfred Lawson, Philip Stanhope, Arthur Ponsonby, W. H. Dickinson, all now forgotten. Ramsay MacDonald is the only exception—a man whom the preparation of these lectures made me rate more highly, to my surprise and even regret.

We can look back in academic detachment and see the explanation for this. Parliament was ceasing to be the direct sounding-board of the nation. The independent member was being squeezed out by the party machine; and it became increasingly unattractive to 'split the party' over foreign affairs as parliament did more and more in domestic legislation. Radical M.P.s swallowed a distasteful foreign policy for the sake of Old Age pensions or the taxation of Land Values. Gladstone had already taken up this attitude when he justified the occupation of Egypt or the annexation of Uganda by referring to Home Rule. The change in the character of parliament influenced him in other ways. During the Crimean war parliament had immediately reflected the national mood, as the triumph of Palmerston showed. In 1876 Disraeli's majority remained unshaken despite the turmoil of agitation over the Bulgarian Horrors. This was Gladstone's justification for going on the stump. Where previously the House of Commons had coerced ministers, now 'the people' had to coerce the House of Commons.

Not only was it more necessary to appeal directly to 'the people'. It was easier; and there were more people to appeal to. More people could read; and this transferred the centre of political decision from the hustings or even the House of Commons to the printed word, until the spoken word had its revenge with radio and television. The politicians lamented this and even tried to prevent it, as they still do. But there was no escape. A man with an intelligent interest in foreign affairs would no longer plod through the columns of *Hansard* (if indeed he ever did); he would certainly not rely on the blue books so carefully edited by the Foreign Office. He would read Brailsford on Macedonia; E. G. Browne on Persia; E. D. Morel on Morocco; Seton-Watson on Hungary; Miss M. E. Durham on Albania. And, one must add, he would be better informed than if he had stuck to official channels. The impact of Dissent was greater, but it was more delayed. Instead of blazing out at once in parliamentary debates, it had to wait for a slow, almost imperceptible change in public opinion—a change which rarely acknowledged its authors.

It was poor consolation to the Dissenters to know that they would win in time, even if they realized it; they were men of conviction, men in a hurry, men who wanted to win now. They were sure that they were advocating the only rational policy. Why did others not respond at once to the voice of Reason? Why were they themselves so obscure? Why was there no new Fox, no Cobden, no Gladstone I am glad to say? They believed, on the whole wrongly, that the Dissenters had been more powerful in the past. This was an old trick. Bright had envied the days of Fox and Burke. Gladstone praised Palmerston in 1894 to the detriment of Rosebery; he even made out that the war scare of 1860 (which he had opposed at the time) had been justified whereas that of 1894 was not. Soon the twentieth-century Dissenters were lamenting the governments of Gladstone— governments which had occupied Egypt, annexed Uganda, threatened Russia with war, and launched the Spencer naval programme.

The Dissenters hit on a simple explanation; or, rather, they emphasized more strongly an explanation which they had always inclined to: foreign policy was a conspiracy, conducted behind the backs of 'the people'. They started with jealousy of the Foreign Office. This was new. Bright and Cobden certainly regard foreign affairs as a conspiracy, but it never occurred to them to suggest that the foreign office conspired, say, against Palmerston. He, too, was in the conspiracy up to the hilt. And of course there was something in it. The permanent officials of the nineteenth century were plain clerks. It is purely a matter of bureaucratic curiosity to know who was Under Secretary in Palmerston's day. In the twentieth century the officials had a real influence on policy from Eyre Crowe to Vansittart. Absurdly enough it became at the end a Dissenting charge against Neville Chamberlain that he was ignoring the permanent officials whom earlier they or their predecessors had so fiercely denounced. Sir Edward Grey was the first foreign secretary to be regarded as the 'prisoner' of his staff. E. D. Morel described him as 'a puppet of his permanent officials . . . a weak man'. Later the affair of the Zinoviev letter seemed to confirm this view of the foreign office; and though MacDonald then defended the professionals, he was ready even in 1928 to denounce 'their winks and their smiles, and their little nudges and their indefinite walkings-out'. The foreign office was supposed to be crammed with guilty secrets. Hence the

G

universal belief between the wars—a view still held by some
—that if only its dreary papers were published, we should
have all sorts of 'revelations'. As a matter of fact nearly
everything can be found out at the time, if you know where
to look for it.

Still the Dissenters did not discriminate sharply between
the professional diplomatists and 'the governing class'. They
held that the party-leaders had made a compact to keep
foreign affairs free from democratic interference. Bertrand
Russell expressed this view in words which Zilliacus still
quoted with approval thirty years later:[1]

In the days of Gladstone and Disraeli, Palmerston and Lord
Derby, Fox and Pitt, Chatham and Lord North, and right back to
the time of the Stuarts, the parties were hotly divided on foreign
policy. . . . 'Continuity' represents no real need of national safety,
but merely a closing up of the ranks among the governing classes
against their common enemy, the people. Ever since 1832, the
upper classes in England have been faced with the problem of retaining as much as possible of the substance of power while abandoning the forms to the clamours of democrats. . . . In foreign
affairs, their ascendancy, threatened by the Manchester School and
Gladstone, was completely recovered twenty years ago [i.e. by
Rosebery], and survived even the collapse of 1906.[2]

Here again there was something in it, though much exaggeration as well. 'Continuity' was openly avowed. The two
front benches accepted in theory a 'national' foreign policy,
though they did not always practise it. Moreover the politics
of the early twentieth century had often the air of a stage
fight despite the violence of public debate. The younger Pitt
entered Brooks's once only in his life; Gladstone and Disraeli
did not frequent the same country houses. But Asquith and
Balfour, Lloyd George and Bonar Law, Churchill and F. E.
Smith, passed many an evening together; and they successfully hushed up scandals which far outdid the *Letters of
Junius* or the satirical imaginings of Hilaire Belloc.

This 'governing-class' foreign policy was, in the Radical

[1] K. Zilliacus, *Mirror of the Past* (1944), p. 128.
[2] Bertrand Russell, *The Foreign Policy of the Entente*, p. 70.

view, essentially aggressive and selfish. A further passage from Bertrand Russell puts this plainly:

The interests of the British democracy do not conflict at any point with the interests of mankind. The interests of the British governing classes conflict at many points with the interests of mankind. . . . A policy of adventure and national prestige appeals most forcibly to the rich, while the wage-earning class, if it understood its own interest and were not caught by the glamour of Jingo phrases, would insist upon a policy of peace and international conciliation.[1]

Though this echoes Cobden, there is a difference of emphasis. All Radicals held that only the governing classes benefited from foreign policy. The old Dissenters meant this literally. Foreign affairs provided the aristocracy with jobs, 'outdoor relief' in Bright's phrase. To quote Bright again, 'the Balance of Power has left us . . . a doubled peerage at one end of the social scale, and far more than a doubled pauperism at the other'. Now the governing classes were extended to include the rich generally. It was Imperialism which produced this change. In the later years of the nineteenth century British history was punctuated by quarrels outside Europe—Egypt in 1882 and afterwards, Angra Pequena in 1884, Siam in 1893, the Kruger telegram in 1896, Fashoda in 1898, repeated alarms in the Far East, the Boer war in 1899. The Balance of Power seemed forgotten. Financiers, not incompetent aristocrats, provided the driving force in foreign policy.

The *Manchester Guardian* described the activities of Cecil Rhodes after the Jameson raid as 'the first memorable and really successful intrusion of a great ring of capitalists into British political discussion'.[2] Keir Hardie wrote of the Boer war:

The war is a capitalist war. The British merchant hopes to secure markets for his goods, the investor an outlet for his capital, the speculator more fools out of whom to make money, and the mining companies cheaper labour and increased dividends.[3]

[1] Russell, *Foreign Policy of the Entente*, p. 71.
[2] 11 May 1896.   [3] William Stewart, *J. Keir Hardie*, p. 151.

It was a great relief to the Radicals when they got Imperialism, their own bastard offspring, from an emotional on to a materialistic basis. They came to regard it as a straight financial swindle, bucket-shop promoting. They did not discriminate between Cecil Rhodes and Horatio Bottomley—both certainly symbols of their epoch. This view is best displayed in Hilaire Belloc's first political novel, *Emmanuel Burden*: the story of how a business man of the old school is captured for a shady imperialist venture by city sharks, their leader of course a Jew.

Just after the Boer war J. A. Hobson, most original and profound of the New Radical writers, put the discussion on a higher plane. He did for Imperialism what Marx had done for capitalism itself: he showed that it sprang from inevitable economic causes, not from the wickedness of individuals. Given Marx's theory of surplus value, the capitalist could not avoid 'robbing the worker at the point of production', however kind he might be as an employer. Given Hobson's theory of under-consumption, the capitalist had to invest his profits abroad, and so became an Imperialist despite his individual pacifism. The export of capital, not the search for raw materials or for markets, caused Imperialism. Hobson put the growth of external investments in one column of figures, the increase of colonial territories in another; and, since they were both going up, argued that the one caused the other. The conclusion may have been faulty. Nevertheless its political influence was enormous. Not only did it shape the outlook of later Dissenters in England. Lenin took over the theory and constructed from it his *Imperialism: the last stage of capitalism*. It was no mean achievement for Hobson to anticipate Keynesian economics with one flick of the wrist and to lay the foundations for Soviet foreign policy with another. No wonder that he never received academic acknowledgement nor held a university chair.

The odd thing about Hobson is that, although he found a Marxist explanation for Imperialism, he did not draw a Marxist conclusion. He was an old-style Rationalist, attending South Place Ethical Church every Sunday and preaching there once a month; and he remained an individualist even when he joined the Labour party much later in life. After showing that Imperialism was inevitable and, from the capitalist's point of view sensible, he condemned it as immoral and stupid. Imperialism was 'a depraved choice of national life'. It appealed 'to the lusts of quantitative acquisition and of forceful domination surviving in a nation from early centuries of animal struggle for existence'.[1] So too the causes of international conflict were 'some . . . the poisonous bye-products of an imperfectly evolving modern industrialism, others are survivors of an obsolescent age of militarism and national isolation'.[2] Capitalists, it seems, would give up Imperialism when they got further away from the caveman. What then became of the implacable statistics which Hobson had displayed? How did the Ethical Church spirit away underconsumption and the search for profitable investment? Hobson did not trouble over this contradiction. He remained firmly of Norman Angell's view that Imperialism and national rivalries were irrational follies, the Great Illusion.

Norman Angell's book, *The Great Illusion*, had a greater immediate influence than Hobson's theories, though it appears more trivial in the long run. Indeed Hobson himself became an avowed Angellite. *The Great Illusion* claimed to destroy the economic argument for war and for Imperialism also. It did not say, as was later alleged, that war was impossible. It proved quite simply that war did not pay. Winning a war brought no advantages; therefore by implication losing a war brought no burdens. Indeed Angell argued that France benefited from paying the indemnity of 1871 and that Germany suffered from receiving it. Nor did Angell shrink from challenging the economic arguments for Imperialism, whether Hobson's or those of the Imperialists. Colonies, he asserted, were an expense, not a source of profit. Often a necessary expense, for annexation of lawless or backward areas opened

[1] The peroration of *Imperialism*.
[2] J. A. Hobson, *The German Panic* (1913), p. 20.

them to trade, as the Imperialists claimed; but to the trade of every country, not merely to that of the Imperial Power. Hence the most rational solution would be a system of international 'mandates' which Hobson himself advocated for China and which became a Radical enthusiasm generally after the first World war. But this did not affect Angell's essential point that sovereignty over a colonial territory brought no gain to the European Power which possessed it. He dismissed with contempt the argument of the Marxist Kautsky that the German capitalists would profit if Germany conquered India:

My critic says the German bankocracy would, in the event of the German conquest of India, divert from England to Germany the profits of the capitalistic exploitation of that possession.

Does he seriously mean by this that the stocks and bonds of Indian railroads, mines, etc., now held by English capitalists would, in the case of the German conquest of India, be confiscated by the German Government and transferred to German capitalists? But he must know that such a thing is impossible, that the danger of financial panic involving all capitalists, German and foreign alike, would be such that the whole influence of German finance would be thrown against such a measure. . . .

Or does the phrase I have quoted mean that the German 'owners' of India would, after the conquest, prevent British capitalists from investing money in India? That, of course, is equally absurd.[1]

This seemed a triumph of reason over economic determinism. In reality it rested on economic determinism of a more primitive kind. 'Angellism' assumed that the laws of economic liberalism were eternal. It supposed that international banking and the gold standard, respect for private property and the sentiment of the Stock Exchange, would survive all upheavals. Of course Angell was not alone in this assumption. It was held even by the worshippers of Power. In 1914 the German general staff expected international trade to continue and therefore refrained from invading Holland; the British government talked earnestly of 'business as usual'.

[1] Norman Angell, *War and the Workers*, p. 36.

Norman Angell thought that he had exploded the Radical view that foreign policy was a conspiracy. There was no conspiracy, only stupidity—a stupidity which extended to the highest places. It was not necessary to carry through a democratic revolution in order to change foreign policy; it was only necessary to explain the real situation to those in power. The Garton foundation which was set up to promote Angell's views kept aloof from politics and distributed to rich men little pamphlets showing that war did not pay. This line was not shared by other Radicals. They managed to believe in the irrationality of international conflict and in 'the conspiracy' at the same time. Hobson, for instance, despite his rationalism, regarded all rich or powerful men as incorrigible and relied on the working classes to bring aggressive foreign policy—indeed all foreign policy—to an abrupt conclusion. He wrote in 1913:

> The organized portion of the working-classes see in the German scare nothing but a familiar move in the high game of politics, by which the employing and possessing classes endeavour to divert the force of popular demands for drastic social reforms by thrusting to the front of the political stage one of the sensational issues of foreign policy kept for that purpose.
> Much can be done if those exposed to their inroads could be instructed in their origins and methods.[1]

For Hobson, too, reason was the decisive cure; but only the working classes were capable of exercising it. Yet the prewar Radicals were remote from 'the democracy' on whom they relied. Their writings were arid, intellectual. The style and arguments of Robert Blatchford, who really wrote for 'the democracy', were repugnant to them. Their periodicals had a coterie air and a small circulation. The *Nation* was subsidized by one Quaker family; E. D. Morel had an annuity from another. The Radicals never envisaged the disappearance of the Liberal party—rather the absorption of the Labour party into it. Massingham wrote in 1909 that 'two organized

---

[1] J. A. Hobson, *The German Panic*, p. 29.

political forces opposed Militarism'. They were 'the British Liberal and Labour parties and Continental Socialism'.[1]

Even more curious, Dissent over foreign affairs, far from pulling the Radicals towards Socialism, pulled the Labour party back towards the Radicals. Foreign affairs sustained the Lib-Lab coalition when social issues at home threatened to divide it. Keir Hardie, for instance, took an independent line on social questions from the moment that he entered parliament in 1892; and he boasted that he was the only 'unwhipped' member in the parliament of 1900. But he kept quiet about foreign affairs until driven to explosion by the Boer war. Then he returned, as it were, to a Radical allegiance. He became a member of the Stop-the-War committee, organized by W. T. Stead, along with non-Socialist Radicals such as Labouchere, Lawson, Philip Stanhope, and Lloyd George. When the war was over he hawked the leadership of the newly-formed Labour party round to Dilke, John Morley, Lloyd George on a plain pro-Boer basis—the implication being that when foreign or imperial affairs predominated, a Socialist had nothing distinctive to say. The Labour party's manifesto for the general election of 1906 devoted one half-sentence to foreign affairs. It was this: 'Wars are fought to make the rich richer; . . .'[2]

Keir Hardie, Ramsay MacDonald and other Labour leaders attended meetings of the Socialist International, where they heard Marxist speeches and even made them: Capitalism was the cause of war; the general strike was the only effective anti-war measure at the moment, International Socialism the only lasting solution. Once back in England, they spoke in purely Radical terms of 'secret diplomacy' and scares 'got up' by armament manufacturers. A little reason, a little enlightenment; and peace would be secure on a basis of international good will. Labour M.P.s certainly spoke a good deal on foreign affairs in the parliament of 1906, though not as much as Dillon the Irish Nationalist. But there

[1] *The Nation*, March 6 1909.
[2] The sentence continues: 'and school children are still neglected.'

was nothing in their speeches to distinguish them from those of middle-class Radicals. I have come across only one Marxist speech in parliament, a speech, that is, stressing financial rivalries as the cause of international conflict. It was made by Baron de Forest, the heir of Baron Hirsch who financed the Orient line; clearly he spoke with some authority. But even de Forest did not advocate the abolition of capitalism. He drew the usual Radical conclusion:

If the people were taken more into the confidence of the Government they would not be willing much longer to set aside their interests for the sake of a few individuals who happen to be of the same nationality. If the cards were laid on the table, I am perfectly certain that the game of international conflict would come to an end.[1]

The Labour party once took an initiative in foreign policy in these years. In January 1911 it held a special party conference at Leicester on disarmament. Emotion predominated, though along with it the appeal to reason that armaments cost a great deal of money. Ramsay MacDonald was in the chair with telling results:

They were the sons and daughters of common men, the children of common folk, the ordinary piece of humanity that the ordinary man had produced, the children of the ordinary family, men and women whose traditions were the tradition of the worker, the wage-earner, the unemployed, the poverty-stricken, the poverty-stricken old, etc. . . . They were going to stretch their hands to their French comrades, to their German comrades, and all other comrades from the North Pole to the South, and from the rising to the setting sun.[2]

Keir Hardie's only contribution was to suggest that 'treaties be subjected to Parliamentary ratification before being signed' —a routine Radical proposal of the time. A proposal to inquire into 'the utility of the strike' was opposed by Henderson and Tom Shaw, and defeated. At the annual conference in 1912 an inquiry into strike action against war was authorized and later made, but with no positive result.

[1] 15 December 1911. *Hansard*, fifth series, xxxii, 2585–91.
[2] Labour party annual report for 1911.

One section of the Labour movement, the smallest, claimed to have a distinctive line in foreign policy. The Social Democratic Federation, later called the British Socialist party, provided the 'tough' element in the movement. Witness Keir Hardie's complaint that there was too much beer at their meetings—the I.L.P. drank tea. The members of the S.D.F. disliked sentimental Radicalism, especially as preached by Keir Hardie and Ramsay MacDonald. They condemned capitalism in intransigent Marxist terms and talked of a general strike, or even revolution, against war. Hyndman, their leader, took this line so long as the discussion was theoretical. But he too was a romantic Radical, though of a more violent French type; and once faced with German militarism, he became an advocate of national defence and of a citizen army, based on universal service. Will Thorne, another member of the S.D.F., moved a resolution in favour of compulsory military service at the Labour party conference in 1909, and was heavily defeated. Robert Blatchford, the Socialist writer of widest appeal, took the patriotic line during the Boer war and turned his pen against the German menace from 1909 onwards. The executive of the Labour party condemned his 'absurd and wicked outburst'. Generally speaking we can agree with the verdict passed by Attlee many years later: 'The Party . . . had no real constructive foreign policy, but shared the views which were traditional in radical circles.'[1]

Let us see then how these traditional Radical views worked out in practical discussion from day to day. Gladstone had demoralized the Radicals, first by his actions, then by his death. Not that all Radicals regretted his disappearance. Labouchere, for instance, disliked Gladstone's campaign over Armenia. He would have let Austria, Russia, and Turkey 'fight it out'—'let us just tell Turkey that we will hope for the success of any revolution or of any Russian interference'. Nevertheless Armenia had provided the one issue that made a stir. The only link of continuity thereafter was a concern for Macedonia, which led to the founding of the Balkan Com-

[1] C. R. Attlee, *The Labour party in Perspective*, p. 200.

mittee, with Bryce as chairman, in 1902. This had an important influence later. The leading members of the Committee
—Brailsford and the two Buxtons—regarded the oppressed
Macedonians as Bulgarians, a view which Brailsford still held
in 1928.[1] They were indignant when most of Macedonia was
acquired by Serbia in 1913 and were therefore ready to sym-
pathize with Austria-Hungary the following year. Here was
the starting-point for the pro-Bulgarian and even pro-
Habsburg attitude which they maintained throughout the
first World war. Moreover in their immediate dealings
with Macedonia they found Lansdowne more receptive of
their complaints than Grey proved to be. This too prepared
them to be critical of Liberal foreign policy.

However, Macedonia was the affair of a few specialists.
There was not enough in it to rekindle Radical enthusiasm.
What brought Radicalism back into a blaze was undoubtedly
the Boer war. Indeed the war created the New Radicalism
which was to triumph in 1906 and which survived, somewhat
attenuated, until the setting up of Lloyd George's Coalition
in 1916. It is sometimes suggested that the Boer war contributed towards the establishment of a separate Labour
party, as shown by the creation of the Labour Representation
Committee in February 1900. On the contrary the war
brought Radicals and Labour men together just when it
looked as if they were going to part. The decisive influence
of the Boer war has a simple explanation. It turned the tables
of morality. Previously the Imperialists had had the best of
the moral argument. The Radicals could argue that Imperialism was expensive, arrogant, interfering. The Imperialists answered by pointing to the abolition of slavery, to
the creation of schools, railways, health-services—in short,
'the British mission'; and the answer was overwhelming.
They tried the same answer during the Boer war when they
asserted that it was being fought for the sake of the native
peoples in South Africa. It was no good. The Imperialists

[1] In *Olives of Endless Age* (1928), Brailsford describes the inhabitants
of Macedonia throughout as 'Bulgarian peasants'.

had the mineowners of the Rand tied securely to their coat-
tails. The war appeared 'a reversion to one of the worst
phases of barbarism . . . contrary to all our ideals of national
political justice'.[1]

Yet the Radicals were curiously hesitant about using the
moral weapon which events had placed in their hands. This
had already been shown in 1896 at the committee of inquiry
into the Jameson Raid. Why did the Radical members fail to
press the inquiry against Chamberlain? Why did they not
insist on the production of the telegrams which, we now
know, must have ruined him and driven him from public life?
Harcourt and Campbell-Bannerman were, maybe, embedded
in the governing ring. But what of Labouchere? Or of Blake,
the Irish Nationalist? Why did they let the opportunity pass?
The mystery will never be solved. So too there were hesitations about the war itself. All Radicals agreed that it was
wrong. Morley put this in imperishable words a few days
before the outbreak of war:

Such a war will bring you no glory. It will bring you no profit
but mischief, and it will be wrong. You may make thousands of
women widows and thousands of children fatherless. It will be
wrong. You may add a new province to your empire. It will still
be wrong. You may give greater buoyancy to the South African
stock and share market. You may create South African booms.
You may send the price of Mr. Rhodes's Chartereds up to a point
beyond the dreams of avarice. Yes, even then it will be
wrong.

But when the war started, Morley withdrew from public life,
claiming that he had better things to do—writing Gladstone's
life in fact. Surely, if the war was wrong, it was desirable that
the Boers should win it? Only the Irish Nationalists drew
this conclusion. They alone cheered the news of British
defeats during Black Week. The I.L.P., led by Keir Hardie,
certainly supported the independence of the Boer republics;
but it wanted to achieve this by a change of heart in England,

[1] Resolution at the Labour party conference, 1901.

not by Boer victories in the field.[1] The Radicals within the Liberal party, Lloyd George and his associates, were valiant against the passions of the time, but they evaded the decisive issue. They were called 'pro-Boers', but they did not deserve the title: they did not desire a Boer victory. They held that British supremacy in South Africa must be asserted once it had been staked—even though staked wrongly. But they also held that the Boers were willing to recognize this supremacy. The war became not so much wrong as unnecessary: all its essential aims could be achieved by negotiation. This was the line which Fox had taken during the war against revolutionary France and which the Dissenters were to take during the first World war. Such a line offered great advantages. Discussion could be brought down to practical details. It was possible to be a Dissenter and a patriot at the same time. But supposing the adversary—French, Boer, or German—was not prepared to recognize essential British interests? What then? Which must be sacrificed—these interests or moral principle? Maybe moderate Boers and moderate British statesmen could have settled things without war, as Lloyd George claimed; maybe the wrongheaded Kruger owed his triumph only to the wrongheadedness of Milner. But what if the Boers were now behind Kruger? The Radicals refused to answer, refused even to contemplate, this question.

Nor did they need to do so. Campbell-Bannerman reunited Radicals and Liberals by a stroke of genius. His attack on 'methods of barbarism' switched the argument from the causes of the war to the way in which it was being conducted. Moral fervour revived free from any awkward moral problems. The Boer war had in the end much the same effect as the Crimean war many years earlier. Its muddles and disappointments discredited not only the competence, but also the principles, of those who had run it. De Wet and his guerrillas ruined Imperialism of the Chamberlain school. And this, too,

[1] The Fabians, incidentally, were enthusiastic for the Boer war, as Bernard Shaw was to be for Mussolini's conquest of Abyssinia many years later.

long before the disaster of 1906. Chamberlain himself left
office; the Unionist remnant in government lost interest in
the 'Milner kindergarten' and merely procrastinated over
self-government for the Transvaal; Ireland was never ruled
with a more generous hand. Foreign affairs showed the same
transformation: the foreign policy of Imperialism crumbled
while Lansdowne was still foreign secretary.

In the great days of Imperialism—say, from the occupation
of Egypt to the Boer war—British policy looked to the Triple
Alliance, and particularly to Germany, for support. It had no
concern for the European Balance of Power; it was shaped by
extra-European rivalries with France and Russia. Salisbury
worked in close co-operation with the Triple Alliance between 1887 and 1892; Rosebery even more closely between
1892 and 1895, despite occasional gestures of irritation. The
climax of this policy was the attempt at a formal alliance with
Germany, which Chamberlain inaugurated in 1898 and which
Lansdowne was still pursuing in 1901. The Radicals abhorred
this policy. Though they disliked all foreign entanglements,
they disliked that with the Triple Alliance most of all. Their
dislike of Austria-Hungary went back to the old days of
Italian unification; their dislike of Germany centred on
Bismarck whom they regarded as the triumphant enemy of
European liberalism. Stead was almost alone in wanting
better relations with Russia; but many Radicals hankered
after 'the liberal alliance' with France, though on a strictly
sentimental basis. This was an unpopular line during the
Imperialist decade of the 'nineties. The *Manchester Guardian*
stood almost alone in preaching conciliation towards France
during the Fashoda crisis.

Suddenly, almost without warning, the Unionist government took over Radical policy. Alliance with Germany was
abandoned; and in April 1904 Lansdowne made the entente
with France. The Radicals were radiant. Hammond's weekly,
the *Speaker*, which originated with the most resolute 'pro-
Boers', wrote lyrically: 'Every Englishman rejoices, and
particularly every Gladstonian Englishman. It is an alliance

which Liberals may foster and develop into a partnership in great causes and splendid memories. Liberalism has found an inspiration in France as Imperialism has found an example in Germany.'[1] Nor did the *Speaker* pretend that the entente had nothing to do with Morocco. Like many Radicals it opposed British Imperialism, but had less objection to the Imperialism of others.

It is to the good and not to the harm of mankind that the great colonizing work in which France is engaged in North-West Africa should be hampered as little as possible. . . . The agreement liberates the energies of France for the undistracted prosecution of a great scheme of enlightened and humane colonization, and for that we rejoice.[2]

The next year the *Speaker* condemned William II's visit to Tangier as 'attempting to foment resistance to one of the most justifiable of all cases of moral pressure on a backward state'; France's right 'cannot be morally challenged by any-one who knows the history of French action in North-West Africa'.[3]

Thus for once the Radicals had no objection to 'con-tinuity' when a Liberal government came in at the end of 1905. On the contrary, they feared that Grey, the old associ-ate of Rosebery and author of the 'Grey declaration' against France in 1895, would repudiate the Anglo-French entente and swing back towards alliance with Germany. Later on it became a grave Radical charge against him that he had com-mitted Great Britain to France by authorizing military con-versations with her. At the time the Radicals were eager to support France; and they would have been delighted if they had known that Grey was prepared to oppose Germany under certain circumstances. The *Speaker* wrote on 13 January 1906:

If Germany is assured that Great Britain and France will act loyally together, there is little likelihood of her forcing a war upon them for Morocco's sake. If Great Britain appears to waver, the

---

[1] The *Speaker*, 16 May, 4 July 1903; 19 August 1905.
[2] The *Speaker*, 16 April 1904.   [3] The *Speaker*, 8 April 1905.

result may be otherwise; and then there could hardly be a worse result for us than a Franco-German war with Great Britain standing on one side.

And on 31 March after the conference at Algeciras: 'German diplomacy has been unsuccessful, that of France entirely open and above-board.'

It would be wrong to argue too strongly from the attitude of a single paper. Hammond stood out in enthusiasm for France and dislike of Germany—'no other Power so steadfastly ignores the conscience of the civilized world'.[1] Scott of the *Manchester Guardian* was always cooler towards France,[2] and more restless about Morocco. Still even he had no objection to the Anglo-French entente so long as it did not develop into a military partnership. The Radicals were happier about foreign policy than they had been within living memory. It seemed the symbol of a secure marriage between Dissent and the Liberal government when Campbell-Bannerman contributed a special article on Disarmament to the first number of the *Nation*, the successor of the *Speaker*.[3] No wonder he was hailed as 'the first Radical Prime Minister'. Yet cracks soon appeared. Before long the Dissenters were fighting fiercely, though ineffectually, against a foreign policy that appeared to them immeasurably evil.

The entente with Russia began the new process of Radical

[1] *The Nation*, 1 June 1907.

[2] Hammond had a delayed triumph over Scott when he wrote pro-French leaders in the *Manchester Guardian* throughout the Second World War. They are collected in *Faith in France* (1944).

[3] Hammond quarrelled with his proprietor early in 1907. The *Speaker* was wound up; and the *Nation* took its place with Massingham as editor. Hammond, I surmise, continued to write leaders for some time. Then he went over to writing history: and was succeeded by Brailsford, who had less enthusiasm for France and less dislike of Germany. These changes were purely a matter of personal accident. Yet they seemed to coincide with a change in Radical outlook; and a historian who did not know of them would be tempted into elaborate generalizations about the intellectual climate. This is a cautionary tale. I have some experience of journalism—perhaps more than befits an academic historian; and I would always look first for personal, accidental factors when trying to study the so-called organs of public opinion.

Dissent. Even Campbell-Bannerman regretted that friendship with Russia coincided with the dissolution of the Duma;
but most Radicals swallowed the business deal of 1907.
Opposition started when the entente developed from business
into sentiment. The Labour party took the lead, and not
only because they were less tied by loyalty to the government. Hostility to Russia was universal in the Socialist
International. French Socialists criticized the Russian alliance;
German Socialists attacked the Russian peril; Russian Socialists denounced tsarist absolutism. For once therefore the
Labour party were keeping in step with their European comrades. Keir Hardie divided the House in protest against
Edward VII's visit to Reval in 1908—a protest repeated
when the tsar came to Cowes the following year. The only
Liberal member who echoed this protest was Arthur Ponsonby—the son of a court official, himself once page to Queen
Victoria; stabbing his own class in the back made him peculiarly unpopular in governing circles. There was a curious
little sequel. Edward VII struck Ponsonby and Keir Hardie
off the list of guests invited to a royal garden party. Hardie
had never attended a garden party and was at first unaware
that he had been excluded. But once knowing of it, he stood
on his rights: 'If I am fit to represent the working classes of
Merthyr, I am fit to attend the garden party at Windsor.'
The Labour party backed him up and asked that the names of
all its members be removed from the lists until Hardie's was
restored. This was, I think, the first occasion when the
Labour party claimed its share in the Establishment from
royal garden parties upwards.

The Dissenting campaign against Russia took a more
practical shape when it turned to defending the liberties of
Persia. For a few years Persia became the principal object of
Radical sympathy—perhaps because in those halcyon days
Persia was virtually the only country in the world where
constitutional liberties were being infringed by a foreign
oppressor. Russia had no longer any Ritualist friends; and
the Persians had the inestimable advantage over the Turks

H

of lacking Christian subjects whom they might massacre. They had a further advantage in their principal English patron, E. G. Browne, who combined scholarship and courage. Russian misdeeds in Persia were repeatedly criticized in the House of Commons, finally provoking a full-scale debate in February 1912. Here again the Labour party took the lead in co-operation with the Irish Nationalists; but a good many Radicals also felt strongly about Persia. Wedgwood complained in 1911: 'You cannot point to one spot from China to Peru where the influence of the Liberal government has made anything better.'[1] As a matter of fact, Grey himself was indignant about Persia, but only in private. In the House he always argued that a division of Persia into spheres of influence was the only means of preventing Russia's absorbing the whole.

The Dissenters did not accept this argument for a moment. They were convinced that there must be some more sinister explanation; and they soon found it. Persia had been sacrificed to 'that foul idol, the Balance of Power'. It was the price paid to Russia for enlisting her against Germany. 'The dread of Germany has tied us to Russia's chariot wheels.'[2] Persia was 'merely a symptom of the Anglo-German situation. . . . The primary consideration of our diplomacy has been to win friendship from Russia and other states as against Germany.'[3] Why had Grey adopted this policy? It could only be the influence of the permanent officials, who enjoyed playing 'the game'. 'We are prisoners of the policy of cornering Germany.' It was inconceivable that a single Power could ever dominate Europe: 'a war such as in the old days gave one side supremacy or material advantage is to-day impossible.'[4] 'The game' of the Balance of Power was being played for its own sake.

[1] 14 December 1911. *Hansard*, fifth series, xxxii, 2624.
[2] *The Nation*, 29 October 1910.
[3] Noel Buxton, 21 February 1912. *Hansard*, fifth series, xxxiv, 691.
[4] G. H. Perris, *Our Foreign Policy and Sir Edward Grey's Failure* (1912), p. 197.

The Dissenters did not start off with any particular affection for Germany. She was praised only in contrast to Russia. Keir Hardie said in 1912: 'If he was called upon to choose between the autocracy of Russia and the present German government he would most unhesitatingly cast his lot on the side of Germany against Russia.'[1] Norman Angell took the same line even in August 1914: 'Russia is only partly civilized, governed by a military autocracy, largely hostile to western ideas of political and religious freedom. Germany on the other hand is . . . highly civilized, with a culture that has contributed greatly in the past to western civilization.'[2] Soon Dissenters were applauding Germany for her own sake. One of them said in 1912: 'There are no greater friends of peace than are the Germans generally. . . . If we want to preserve the permanent peace of Europe, the best nation with whom we could join would be Germany.'[3] Nevertheless the Dissenters knew little of Germany at first hand. Noel Buxton, for instance, perhaps Grey's most influential critic within the Liberal party, never visited Berlin until the Agadir crisis in the summer of 1911. The Dissenters took up Germany simply because she was being 'penned in'. They were more hostile to the Foreign Office than favourable to Germany.

Relations with Germany became the paramount issue in politics with the great naval scare of 1909. This affair put the Dissenters in a quandary. They had always supported maritime supremacy, at any rate in theory. As the *Westminster Gazette* wrote years before (1893): 'From Cromwell to Cobden good Radicals have ever insisted on an all-powerful Navy.' Even now the Radicals held that 'we must maintain much the best and strongest fleet': and most of them blamed Germany for starting the race. But they also held, in their usual way, that British supremacy could be maintained without any increased expenditure. Indeed every organization from the National Liberal Federation downwards called for a

[1] Labour party conference, 1912.
[2] Norman Angell, *After All* (1952), p. 183.
[3] W. H. Dickinson, 25 July 1912. *Hansard*, fifth series, xli, 1470.

reduction in the naval estimates; and the same demand was strongly pressed inside the Cabinet. One Cabinet Minister carried the campaign to the public platform. To preach an inevitable antagonism between England and Germany, he declared, was 'a repudiation not only of the whole message of Liberalism, but of the very structure of civilization'. The panic had been caused by 'the vicious activity of a few men . . . a false lying panic started in the party interests of the Conservatives'. 'We live in a period of superficial alarms, when it is thought patriotic and statesmanlike, far-seeing, clever and Bismarckian to predict hideous and direful wars as imminent. . . . Happily for the world, war is not coming.' These were the judgements of Winston Churchill.

The Liberal government handled its tactics well. In March 1909 it stood out against the Tory cry of 'we want eight and we won't wait', and won the united support of its followers for a proposal to build four dreadnoughts with four 'contingent' ships which might be authorized later. Soon after, the Liberals were resoundingly defeated in a bye-election at Croydon—the exact equivalent in reverse of the election at East Fulham in 1934. Most Liberal M.P.s heeded the warning; and only seventy-nine went into the No lobby when on an alarm of German acceleration the four contingent ships were authorized in July.

It is far from my purpose to disentangle the facts in this great alarm. We cannot decide whether German acceleration was deliberate until someone examines the archives of the German Navy—now, I believe, rigorously guarded at Admiralty House. But there is one point of some interest. Mr. Mulliner of the Coventry Electric Boat Company claimed to have supplied the information on which the alarm was based. The Admiralty resented his claim and refused to grant contracts to his firm while he remained on the board. He lost his post; and carried his complaints to the public Press. His claims were, I think, exaggerated. No matter, they were made. Mr. Mulliner became for thirty years afterwards the principal witness against 'the arms-traffic'. F. W. Hirst,

editor of the *Economist*, henceforth attributed all international conflicts to 'armour-plate'. He did this in his paper,
in *The Six Panics* (1913)—a pamphlet much inferior to
Cobden's *The Three Panics* on which it was modelled—even
in a book published in 1937.[1] Snowden took the same line in
the House of Commons in March 1914. So did Walton New-
bold, a pupil of Professor Tout and later the first Communist
M.P., in *How Europe Armed for War*. In the nineteen-thirties
a Senate Committee of Inquiry in the United States and a
Royal Commission in this country both condemned the private
manufacture of armaments. The substantial, unshakable witness was still Mr. Mulliner. It would have saved historians
as well as politicians a great deal of trouble if the Admiralty
had ordered a few Electric Boats, whatever they may
be.

It is often said that British antagonism towards Germany
became established with the naval scare of 1909 and then
mounted steadily until the outbreak of war in 1914. This is a
grave distortion, the sort of telescoping of events which
comes with hindsight. The naval scare involved Germany
almost by accident—the accident that she was building a great
fleet. The naval race was regarded as an interruption, un-
happy but pointless, in what were otherwise good relations.
These relations improved again once the decision had been
taken to win the race; and the Dissenters appeared the more
vindicated when the prophecies of German acceleration
turned out to be a false alarm. 1910 was a year of Anglo-
German detente; and early in 1911 Grey averted a Radical
motion to reduce the naval estimates only by accepting an
American proposal for general arbitration. The Agadir crisis
blew up out of a clear sky. War between England and Germany seemed a serious possibility for the first time. Dissent
became more general; and now Liberals led—the Labour
party was content to follow. Noel Buxton, whose interests
had hitherto been confined to Macedonia, was the new
leader; and he organized a somewhat ineffectual attack on

[1] F. W. Hirst, *Armaments: the race and the crisis* (1937).

Grey's foreign policy in November 1911 when the crisis was over.

More important, the Agadir crisis provoked the first attempts in the twentieth century at the organization of Dissent against the official line of foreign policy. The Foreign Affairs Group of the Liberal party in parliament was set up. It had seventy-odd members who met regularly and tried to plan a concerted campaign. Noel Buxton, its originator, was mainly concerned to meet 'the legitimate aspirations of Germany'—a phrase which he took, oddly enough, from a speech by Asquith at the Mansion House. Ponsonby, the other leading member, had a more general grievance against secret diplomacy. Their first statement of principle combined the two ideas. 'Policy is virtually dictated by a very small number of permanent men at the Foreign Office. . . . It is obvious that . . . the friction with Germany has been partly due to the private opinions of some of our diplomatists.'[1]

The Dissenters also carried their campaign outside parliament by setting up the Foreign Policy Committee, under the presidency of Lord Courtney of Penwith. Courtney certainly had an impeccable Dissenting record. Originally a Conservative, he went over to Gladstone at the time of the Bulgarian Horrors; next broke with Gladstone over Home Rule; and then broke with the Unionists over the Boer war. Now he regarded the Agadir crisis as simply an affair of 'coal depots':

That Germany desires to acquire and is bound to acquire coaling stations here and there is one of the phases of the inevitable. It depends upon the manifestation of our temper in respect of such acquisitions whether they would remain merely mercantile stations or would be converted into naval bases.[2]

The Foreign Policy Committee, too, demanded 'a friendly approach to the German Government', and 'greater publicity as to foreign affairs and fuller Parliamentary control of

[1] T. P. Conwell-Evans, *Foreign Policy from a Back Bench*, p. 82.
[2] Courtney to Grey, 5 September 1911. G. P. Gooch, *Lord Courtney of Penwith*, p. 567.

the main lines of policy'. The Committee started with a bang, Philip Morell's money, and R. C. K. Ensor as secretary. But it never got going. It was perhaps too tied to the Radical intellectuals, and lacked the mass support that it might have got from associating with Labour men. Most of all, it lacked a dynamic leader.

Yet he was waiting in the wings; he, too, drawn into foreign affairs by Agadir. He was E. D. Morel. I shall have more to say of him in my next lecture when I come to the years of his historic success; but he must be introduced now. In 1911 Morel had just carried to a triumphant conclusion the campaign against atrocities in the Belgian Congo—that campaign of which Grey said: 'No question has so stirred the country for thirty years', that is, since the Bulgarian Horrors. The campaign ended with a presentation to Morel by the Congo Committee on 29 May 1911; it was a stroke of luck for him that the *Panther* moored off Agadir barely a month later. Morel was the first Radical of the twentieth century who took up foreign affairs as a whole-time interest. He was not distracted by Ireland or social reform or women's rights; like Urquhart, he worked with the Radicals solely because they accepted his views on foreign affairs. He resembled Urquhart in other ways. He had sublime confidence in his own judgement and never shrank from attributing base motives to others. He wrote in 1917:

I would never recognize Asquith or Lloyd George, or Grey or Churchill as my chiefs to whom I owed allegiance. They are dishonest. . . . Is there a chance for really honest men to play a part, *determining the destinies* of a country which allows itself to be run by such fifth rate men as Milner, Smith, Churchill, Carson, Henderson?

And again in 1920, when he became parliamentary candidate for Dundee:

I look upon Churchill as such a personal force for evil that I would take up the fight against him with a whole heart.[1]

[1] These and other passages from Morel's papers are derived from a thesis by R. Wuliger in the library of London University.

Morel was often described as a pro-German, or even as a German agent. This was untrue. He was half-French by birth, almost wholly French by upbringing; and his uncompromising outlook would have been less surprising in a French journalist. He was certainly unscrupulous in his means —perhaps also a French trait. His first great pamphlet, *Morocco in Diplomacy*, was subsidized by the Albert Committee, which got its money from Theodore Rhodes, British manager of North German Lloyd. The Congo campaign had already made Morel hostile to Grey; and he had detected an Anglo-French partnership to protect Belgium. Against this he wished to invoke German help. The Congo, he thought, should have been 'a golden bridge' between England and Germany. Once convinced that British policy was wrong, he became equally convinced that German policy was right. He stated the German case so uncompromisingly during the war that Bertrand Russell, Fenner Brockway, and Lowes Dickinson all warned him not to overdo it; and the German Social Democrats themselves sent a message through Bertrand Russell that Morel was embarrassing them in the campaign against their own government. Morel was not shaken by these expostulations.

Morel first stepped on to the stage in November 1911 when the secret clauses of the Anglo-French entente were published. *Morocco in Diplomacy* (later extended as *Ten Years of Secret Diplomacy*) had an influence without parallel. Ramsay MacDonald said of it: 'From that time I suspected our diplomacy, and ceased to believe the assurances given by Ministers in parliament or out of it.' Secret diplomacy had always been condemned; but now the case against it was made from the documents of the diplomatists themselves. All the later studies of 'war-origins' stem from Morel's pamphlet; and the interwar historians were as much cut from his cloak as the Russian novelists, according to Turgenev, were from Gogol's. Morel caused more than a change of method; he caused a change of outlook. Previously the Radicals had looked affectionately at 'the liberal alliance' with France, however much they disliked the entente with Russia. Now France, too, was branded as an Imperialist power; and the entente cordiale, which the Radicals had welcomed as their own conception, appeared in retrospect as a sordid colonial bargain, from which sprang all subsequent evils. Later on, the Anglo-French entente was even regarded as the principal cause of the first World war. Morel wrote in 1919:

The genesis of the recent war lay . . . in the secret bargain which sought to consolidate British power in Egypt . . . by handing over Morocco to France and by the determination arrived at, without the knowledge of our people, to support that secret bargain at the risk of promoting a war of the world.[1]

Men often interpret their own past in the light of later knowledge; and the Radicals soon believed that they had opposed the Anglo-French entente from the beginning.

The crisis of Agadir seemed to imply that a new wave of Imperialism had begun, or perhaps that Imperialism had never ceased. English Dissenters were agreed that it was a crisis of imperial expansion, not of the European balance. There was nothing at stake in Europe. 'Its map is fixed. . . . European hearths and homes were never in danger. . . . The question is no longer whether Austria shall oppress a European race in Lombardy, or whether the Rhine shall be German. . . . Policy is busied in reality over Moroccan iron-ore, Persian railways, and the problematic crops of Mesopotamia.'[2] The danger was not war, but 'the ruinous game of a dry war, a bloodless duel, a battle of steel and gold'.[3] Once accept this analysis, and profound consequences followed. England, France and Russia had made the greatest territorial gains outside Europe; clearly therefore they were the most aggressive Powers. Germany had gained least; therefore she was the most pacific—as well as the most justly aggrieved. The further development of the argument took one of two forms. According to the cruder view, the 'imperialist

[1] *Diplomacy Revealed* (1919), xxvi.
[2] *The Nation*, 14 January, 8 April 1911.
[3] *The Nation*, 2 September 1911.

brigands of the Entente' were now set on war in order to make yet more colonial gains; the sophisticated view saw them as satiated Powers, concerned only to hold what they had, but, in the long perspective of history, more guilty than Germany all the same. By either version, Germany, once 'the natural ally' of the Imperialists, now won Radical sympathies. The change was never complete. Many Radicals retained a sentimental regret for France; and 'the liberal alliance' could sometimes be revived. Englishmen regarded France as the Imperialist Power *par excellence* only after the defeat of Germany in the nineteen-twenties. Still the first sketch of this picture was drawn by Morel in the autumn of 1911. Henceforth the Triple Entente as a whole, and not merely the entente with Russia, stood condemned in Radical eyes.

Morel himself cared little for diagnosis. He was content to describe particular crimes. The wickedness of the rich and powerful was explanation enough for him. In old Radical fashion, he blamed aristocratic government and secret diplomacy more than the economic system. For a Marxist analysis, expressed in English Radical terms, we must look to Brailsford's book, *The War of Steel and Gold*, which—though published only in March 1914—reflected the outlook of the years immediately before the war. Its doctrine was not new. Brailsford merely applied Hobson's theory of 1902 that Imperialism sprang from the search for profitable investment overseas. Hobson had dealt only with British Imperialism. Brailsford ranged over all the European Powers. He was convinced that the leaders of 'finance capitalism' controlled the policy of their respective states. But he was also convinced that these leaders were rational, though wicked, men, who subordinated everything to their financial advantage. Hence he arrived at a surprisingly cheerful conclusion: though the financiers would dispute with their rivals, they would never go to war. He wrote early in 1914:

The dangers which forced our ancestors into European coalitions and Continental wars have gone never to return. . . . It is as certain as anything in politics can be, that the frontiers of our modern national states are finally drawn. My own belief is that there will be no more wars among the six Great Powers.[1]

Even the outbreak of war did not shake Brailsford's confidence in the truth of his analysis. The third edition of *The War of Steel and Gold*, published in 1915, silently omitted the last sentence I have just quoted, but added in the preface: 'It seems to me doubtful whether [questions of nationality] could have made a general war, had not colonial and economic issues supplied a wider motive for the use of force.'[2] And more strongly in the postscript:

War could never have come about save for these sordid colonial and economic issues. . . . France is defending her colonies and especially Morocco. Germany is attacking and the Allies are maintaining the present distribution of colonies and dependencies. The stakes lie outside Europe, though the war is fought on its soil.[3]

By 1915 Brailsford could only lament and denounce. Before the war he offered also a remedy. The capitalists of every country cared only for profit; they would therefore remain peaceful if the profits offered were large enough. There should be capitalist partnerships instead of capitalist rivalries —the 'consortium' which Hobson had hoped for in China. England and Germany were the leading capitalist Powers; therefore they should make a deal. They should divide the Portuguese colonies and share the Bagdad railway. If this deal were extended to Persia, and if France too 'opened her Money Market to Germany', all problems of foreign policy would be solved. Germany, now a contented Power, would 'apply an ungrudging policy of conciliation to Alsace-Lorraine';[4] and the three Western Powers would present a united front against Russia, 'today the restless and incalculable factor in the European system'.[5] These ideas did not

[1] H. N. Brailsford, *The War of Steel and Gold* (1914), p. 35.
[2] Brailsford, *The War of Steel and Gold*, third edition (1915), p. 7.
[3] Brailsford, *The War of Steel and Gold*, third edition, p. 338.
[4] *The Nation*, 24 May 1913.   [5] *The Nation*, 30 May 1914.

have to wait for *The War of Steel and Gold* for their formulation. They were first worked out in a series of articles on 'The Trend of Foreign Policy' which *The Nation* published in May and June 1912—articles which represented a collaboration between Brailsford and Hobson, or which perhaps Brailsford wrote after absorbing Hobson's economic teaching.

The Agadir crisis, and the ideas which sprang from it, gave Radicalism a more up-to-date look. Radicalism between 1906 and 1911 had been old-fashioned, as of course some of it remained: quotations from Bright against the Balance of Power; attacks on secret diplomacy; moral indignation against Russia which harked straight back to the outcry over Poland seventy years before. The only Radical demand was Isolation, or more truly the 'no foreign politics!' which Cobden had preached. Now the Radicals had a constructive alternative, attuned to the materialistic spirit of the age. Previously they had accused Grey of sacrificing Persia and Morocco for the sake of the Balance of Power; now it appeared that he had endangered European peace for the sake of Persia and Egypt. Grey's flaw was revealed: despite his high moral tone, he was still a Liberal Imperialist. The Radicals revived all their suspicions of the Boer war. Loreburn, Lord Chancellor, said in 1911: 'Always remember that this is a Liberal League Government.'[1] And Noel Buxton in July 1912: 'The spirit which promoted the Boer war is the spirit which is concerned in the present question of Anglo-German relations.'[2] The Radicals wished to satisfy 'the legitimate aspirations of Germany'; and they knew what these aspirations were—Angola, the Bagdad railway, Persia, China, the 'consortium' everywhere. Even the Labour party did not quarrel with this programme so long as it was conducted with public funds. Ramsay MacDonald for instance welcomed the purchase of shares in Anglo-Persian Oil by the British government as 'something of a socialist experiment'.[3]

[1] J. L. Hammond, *C. P. Scott*, p. 153.
[2] *Hansard*, fifth series, xl, 2006.   [3] *Hansard*, fifth series, lxiii, 1160.

National independence and economic freedom were, it seems, Not For Export: even the Socialist International was virtually limited to Europe. There was one honourable exception. Bertrand Russell wrote:

The only hope for Persia, as for the rest of Asia, seems to lie in such a weakening of all the Great Powers of Europe [in war] as shall enable the more backward nations to throw off the yoke fastened on them by the Cabinets and financiers of 'civilized' States.[1]

The Radicals had for the first time a practical and effective policy. Yet at this very moment their Dissent faded away. They had divided the House over Persia in 1908 and 1909, over armaments in 1908 and 1911. They staged a grandiose attack on Grey after Agadir.[2] Thereafter they fell silent. The Foreign Policy Committee dissolved unnoticed. The other Dissenting organizations—the Anglo-German Friendship Society, the Balkan Committee, the Society of the Friends of Russian Freedom, the Anglo-Russian Committee, the Persia Committee—all lapsed into obscurity. This seems a paradox. But there is a simple explanation: the Dissenters had won. Grey adopted their policy. They said they had a cure for international tension; he applied it. He joined Germany in the Bagdad railway concession, and agreed to divide the Portuguese colonies with her. He brought the military and naval talks with France before the Cabinet, and, with its approval, told the French that these talks did not constitute 'an engagement that commits either Government to action in a contingency that has not arisen and may never arise'.[3] He resisted the Russians more strenuously in Persia; and the Anglo-Persian Oil company made a deal with German interests against Russian and American competitors. Most of all, during the Balkan wars, Grey seemed to abandon the Balance of Power and to revive the Concert of Europe. *The*

[1] Bertrand Russell, *The Foreign Policy of the Entente*, p. 63.
[2] Persia: 4 June 1908, 53–270; 22 July 1909, 79–187; armaments: 7 March 1908, 73–320; 13 March 1911, 56–276; post-Agadir: 27 November and 14 December 1911.   [3] Grey to Cambon, 22 November 1912.

Nation wrote triumphantly: 'The credit belongs in equal parts to the statesmen of Germany and Sir Edward Grey. They have found at last a consciousness of their common duties. . . There might evolve from this temporary association some permanent machinery of legislation.'[1] And Grey was in fact moving towards some arrangement which would guarantee Germany against France as well as France against Germany.

International relations seemed turned upside down. The Triple Entente was dissolving; the partnership of 'western humanity' just round the corner. The *Nation* wrote truly on 15 December 1913: 'Nothing more than a memory is left of the old Anglo-German antagonism.' Lloyd George resisted the naval estimates for 1914 with Radical backing;[2] and he greeted the New Year with a message that there was 'a spread of revolt against military oppression' throughout the whole of Christendom, and particularly throughout the whole of Western Europe.[3] His confidence increased with the passing of the months. Speaking of Anglo-German relations in the House of Commons on 23 July 1914 he said: 'The two great Empires begin to realize that they can co-operate for common ends, and that the points of co-operation are greater and more numerous and more important than the points of possible controversy.'[4] Looking back afterwards, the Radicals came to believe that Grey had cheated them: he had talked peace while preparing for war. They were wrong. Grey was much nearer in outlook to the Radicals than he was to Eyre Crowe or Arthur Nicolson of the Foreign Office. He defended his permanent officials loyally; and he was sometimes impatient with Radical critics. But he believed, as they did, that Germany had genuine economic grievances and that these should be met. He believed perhaps more than they did that 'fear will haunt our gates, until we have organized an

---

[1] *The Nation*, 10 May 1913.

[2] The Radicals prepared to campaign against estimates rumoured to be £56,000,000. £50,000,000 was the top figure that they were willing to accept. But they acquiesced when the estimates were reduced to £51,000,000.

[3] *Daily Chronicle*, 1 January 1914.   [4] *Hansard*, fifth series, lxv, 727.

international system of security and order'.[1] It did not need the Great War to turn Sir Edward Grey into an advocate for the League of Nations.

I confess that this conclusion surprised me. We interpret past events in the light of what happened later; and it is difficult, perhaps impossible, to see the past as it was at the time. We like to think that history runs only one way, that great events have great causes. The first World war changed the destiny of civilization; therefore we believe that its coming was long announced. It would be humiliating to admit that the outbreak of war was an accident. Certainly there was tension in the international relations of 1914; the British Expeditionary Force was prepared, and the Navy at the height of its power. Yet there was a real relaxation as well as real tension. The Radicals believed, rightly, that Grey was following their policy; and he believed that this policy was succeeding. This explains why he allowed the ambassadors' conference to dissolve; it explains why the Dissenters remained so quiet and accepted so readily Grey's misleading denial of a naval agreement with Russia; it explains why nobody in England worried about the assassination of Franz Ferdinand at Sarajevo. Serbia had no friends in England, and Austria-Hungary few enemies. Most Balkan experts were 'Bulgarian'; even Seton-Watson was more Czech and Croat than Serb. Austria had universal suffrage and a strong Social Democrat party, altogether a more enlightened country than Russia. 'We think Austria the better and more civilizing influence.'[2] Even after the outbreak of war the *Nation* described Serbia as 'the basest member of the European family'.[3]

When the crisis exploded on 28 July, the choice seemed between Russia and Germany, not between Russia and Austria-Hungary. Dissenters of every school gave an emphatically anti-Russian answer. Not only did they regard Russia as more at fault in this particular conflict; she seemed to them the greater danger to civilization and to the British

[1] *The Nation*, 14 March 1914.   [2] *The Nation*, 1 August 1914.
[3] *The Nation*, 8 August 1914.

empire. Norman Angell launched the Neutrality League and declared on 28 July: 'If we are successful in securing the victory of Russia . . . we shall upset the balance enormously, by making her the dominant military power in Europe.' E. D. Morel wrote on 4 August: 'Our intervention means an intervention on behalf of Russian despotism against a German civilization so akin to our own. . . . We shall have contributed to raise against ourselves a Power which later on it will tax our utmost resources to cope with, not in Europe only, but in Asia—especially in Asia.' Arnold Rowntree said much the same in the House on 3 August: 'When we go to war against Germany, we go to war against a people who, after all, hold largely the ideals which we hold.'[1] *The Nation*, his organ, echoed this a fortnight later when it was wholeheartedly supporting the war: 'A Russian hegemony would be an even graver menace to European liberties than the German supremacy which is almost certainly ended for ever.'[2] It may be said that these Dissenters had been persistently pro-German. But even Hyndman, who was eager for war against Germany, could find only this grudging justification on 12 August: 'As matters stand today it is a choice of evils. . . . The victory of Germany would be worse for civilization and humanity than the success of the Allies.'

It is not surprising that the Radicals opposed going to war; and even less surprising that they were confident of success. The *Nation* wrote rightly on 1 August: 'There has been no crisis in which the public opinion of the English people was so definitely opposed to war as the present moment.' Lloyd George said the same from inside the Cabinet on 27 July: 'There could be no question of our taking part in any war in the first instance. I know of no Minister who would be in favour of it.'[3] Some members of the Cabinet, such as Herbert Samuel, claimed later that they had sat tight and said nothing in the firm belief that, when the question of Belgium came up, it would provide the answer of itself. I doubt it. I am

[1] *Hansard*, fifth series, lxv, 1846.   [2] *The Nation*, 15 August 1914.
[3] J. L. Hammond, *C. P. Scott*, p. 177.

inclined to think that for a few days the Liberal government hoped to restore its waning popularity by keeping out of war, as their American prototype, Woodrow Wilson, did until 1917. The popularity was certainly waiting for them: great meetings in London, Manchester and elsewhere, eighty-one members of Cambridge University prepared to sign a letter to *The Times*—the first demonstration, by the way, of the special Cambridge contribution to Dissent which was to bulk large during the war.

The change of attitude on 3 August, the swing to enthusiastic support for war, was not a gradual process; it was a revolution. The choice was no longer between Germany and Russia, but between Germany and France; and the Radicals responded to the old call of 'the liberal alliance'. The threat to Belgium made the change easier; but it merely pushed the Radicals through a door that was already open. Grey's speech of 3 August which carried all before it has little about Belgium compared with the general argument in regard to France. Grey himself had not foreseen the revolution of feeling: he went down to the House expecting to be disowned by his party and prepared to resign. It was a stroke of luck that no Imperialist issue was involved, no mention of Morocco or of Persia. Fundamentally contemporaries saw the overriding fact which was afterwards obscured by many ingenious arguments: whatever the rights and wrongs of the Sarajevo assassination or of Russia's mobilization or, more broadly, of the Franco-Russian alliance, the war came about solely because Germany declared war on France and Russia. Ensor, himself a pre-war Dissenter, expressed their view many years later: 'The liberals had been making it an article of party faith that militarist Germany was not so black as it was painted. Now in a flash it seemed to them self-revealed as much blacker.'[1]

I have been speaking in these last few paragraphs solely of the Dissenters within the Liberal party. The record of the Labour party is of peculiar interest. Labour was, of course,

[1] R. C. K. Ensor, *England 1870–1914*, p. 575.

I

resolutely anti-Russian. On 2 August the British section of the International Socialist Bureau, which spoke for all sections of the Labour movement, declared: 'The success of Russia at the present day would be a curse to the world.' Ramsay MacDonald, leader of the parliamentary party, still took this line when he spoke after Grey on 3 August. But the Labour party also tried to face the French side of the problem. On 5 August the Executive resolved: 'The conflict was owing to Foreign Ministers pursuing diplomatic policies for the purpose of maintaining a balance of power; our own policy of understandings with France and Russia was only bound to increase the power of Russia both in Europe and Asia and to endanger good relations with Germany.' Here was the basis for a future policy of Dissent. But the parliamentary party would have none of it. The Labour M.P.s rejected the resolution of their own Executive.

Only four M.P.s, all belonging to the I.L.P., voted for the Executive's resolution. One of the four was Ramsay Mac-Donald, who resigned as leader of the parliamentary party. Yet MacDonald was neither a pacifist nor a revolutionary Marxist. His outlook had seemed indistinguishable from that of the Radicals; and he declared that he would support the war if he thought that this country or France were in real danger. Why did he condemn himself to years of unpopularity in the company of extremists whose outlook he did not really share? Fenner Brockway, himself one of these extremists, thought that it was bad timing: that MacDonald had hoped to capture the Radical leadership. Imagine his position, if he had been supported by the *Manchester Guardian*, *The Nation*, the *Daily News*, the *Economist*, the National Liberal Federation, to say nothing of eight or ten members of the Cabinet. He had been going with the tide until 3 August, and then had failed to jump clear in time. It is possible. Men make catastrophic mistakes and benefit from them later to their own astonishment. But it is also possible that MacDonald sensed, with the instinct of a great leader, that sooner or later Dissent would revive. After all, what could he gain from supporting the war? At most a subordinate position in the government; perhaps President of the Board of Education, which is what Henderson, his successor, got a little later. Adhering to his present line meant unpopularity and isolation. But it gave him the one chance of defeating Lloyd George, his predestined rival for the leadership of Radical-Socialism. MacDonald gambled on a great scale when he stuck to his convictions; and the gamble paid off. Lloyd George became Prime Minister and The Man who won the War; but it ruined him in the end and he was excluded from office for the last twenty years of his life. MacDonald was to see the Labour party under his leadership the largest single party in the House; himself Prime Minister for longer than Lloyd George and ultimately indeed, though under strange circumstances, with a greater majority than any British Prime Minister has known in peace-time. This was the fruit of his abortive Dissent on 5 August 1914.

V

THE GREAT WAR

THE TRIUMPH OF E. D. MOREL

BEFORE 1914 everyone expected that a great European war, if it came, would be decided in the first few weeks. And so it was, though in strange ways. Winston Churchill has written of the battle of the Marne: 'The War was decided in the first twenty days of fighting, and all that happened afterwards consisted in battles which, however formidable and devastating, were but desperate and vain appeals against the decision of Fate.'[1] 5 September was the eve of the Marne; the day also of an event unnoticed at the time that was equally decisive. For it determined that the verdict of war would not be permanent. This event was the founding of the Union of Democratic Control. The U.D.C. succeeded where the Foreign Policy Committee and all its other predecessors had failed. Not only did it establish itself. It launched a version of international relations which gradually won general acceptance far beyond the circle of those who knew that they were being influenced by the U.D.C. Mrs. Swanwick, one of its founders, tells how a Trade Union branch in 1915 passed unanimously a resolution on war aims; and then, on someone pointing out that this reflected the policy of the U.D.C., as unanimously rescinded it. Later on, the resolutions were to be passed, and there was no rescinding.

The Union of Democratic Control sprang from the scattered remnant who had opposed Grey's policy on 3 August. By no means all of them. Morley withdrew from public life, replying to every inquiry with Cobden's words during the Crimean war that he would never again open his

[1] Churchill, preface to E. L. Spears, *Liaison, 1914*, p. vii.

mouth while a war was on. John Burns was also silent, though he voted with the 'peace' minority in 1916 and 1917. Many of the Radical journalists who had criticized Grey now supported the war, at any rate until 1917. C. P. Scott, of the *Manchester Guardian*, always lived in the present, and was more concerned to win the war than to go back over the past. By an agreeable irony, the Union—devoted to the attack on secret diplomacy—itself began with a private appeal to individuals, and was flushed into the open only by an unauthorized publication of this appeal in the pro-war Press. Four members of parliament were in at the foundation of the U.D.C.: two Radicals, Ponsonby and Charles Trevelyan, and two from the I.L.P., Ramsay MacDonald and Fred Jowett of Bradford.[1] But the M.P.s counted for less than the intellectuals: Hobson, Norman Angell, Bertrand Russell; they were soon joined by Lowes Dickinson, Fellow of King's College, Cambridge. More important still, the Union got E. D. Morel as secretary. In the words of Mrs. Swanwick, its historian: 'E.D.M. was the U.D.C., and the U.D.C. was E.D.M.'

Morel has never had an equal as organizer and leader of a Dissenting movement. He knew exactly where to look for rich sympathizers; and he took money from them without weakening the democratic character of the Union. Millionaires and factory workers alike accepted his leadership. He knew, too, exactly what was wrong in foreign policy and what should be done instead. He was more than a critic; in his own mind, he was from the first the alternative foreign secretary, the foreign secretary of Dissent. He never left his followers at a loss. Morel saw sharply, clearly, dogmatically. Thanks to him, the Dissent of the war years did not wander complainingly in the void; though a minority, it spoke with a resolute voice. Morel's own writings dealt with pre-war

[1] Keir Hardie, though a Dissenter of the first hour, was too discouraged by the desertion of his former supporters to make a new effort. He died of a broken heart in September 1915. Philip Snowden was in the Antipodes and returned only in November. He then became an active Dissenter in parliament, but was less closely associated with the U.D.C., perhaps because MacDonald was prominent in it.

diplomacy in detail, and offered an immediate policy in the present; there was no vague talk of waiting for the Socialist revolution or a change of heart. Not that Morel shunned general disquisitions. For these he turned to the outstanding intellectuals among his associates: Hobson, Brailsford, Bertrand Russell, Lowes Dickinson, Dr. G. P. Gooch.

The Union of Democratic Control had a powerful offshoot in Cambridge, which became a home of intellectual Dissent while Oxford specialized in emotional uplift, supporting the war. The group which had one foot in Cambridge and the other in Bloomsbury was solidly determined to remain sane when all the world was mad. Bertrand Russell wrote a pamphlet against *The Foreign Policy of the Entente*; was imprisoned on a charge of interfering with recruiting; and was deprived of his lectureship at Trinity as a result. You must remember that the civilian enthusiasts for the first World war developed a hysteria almost wholly absent in the second. Lowes Dickinson invented two phrases that were to ring round the world: 'the League of Nations' and 'the international anarchy'. Leonard Woolf, who had married Virginia Stephen, devised one of the first schemes for 'International Government'. Clive Bell wrote early in 1915 a pamphlet, *Peace at Once*, which I have not managed to see. Lytton Strachey, when before a Tribunal, gave the most famous and telling answer ever made to the question: 'What would you do if you saw a German attempting to violate your sister?' One of the Bloomsbury set was out of Cambridge. He was a high official at the Treasury, and remained at his desk even when his friends became conscientious objectors. In atonement he took 'a solemn pledge' to himself that he would build a better world—a pledge that he kept with devastating effect in 1919. He was J. M. Keynes.

The most sensational stroke of this group was to take over *The Cambridge Magazine*, which had started in 1912 as a brighter rival of *The Cambridge Review*. Now academical trivialities took second place; and the *Magazine* gave a dazzling display of Dissent at its most aridly intellectual level.

Mrs. Dorothy Buxton, member of a famous Cambridge family, contributed a weekly survey of the foreign Press, which was designed to show that there were plenty of sane and moderate men in enemy countries. This survey became so popular that it had to be continued during vacations as an independent supplement. The *Magazine* had other weapons. Adelyne More, that eccentric female, was one of the gayest ironists since Swift. This was not surprising since her name disguised, though it could hardly conceal, C. K. Ogden, the *Magazine's* editor. Rarely has a University periodical achieved national importance of this kind, at any rate since the decline of theological dispute.

The Union of Democratic Control had however another side. It accepted membership from organizations as well as from individuals; and most of these bodies were working-class—trade union branches, co-operative societies, branches of the I.L.P., women's sections of the Labour party. As Mrs. Swanwick puts it: 'The appeal was from the first direct to the workers. . . . They believe in a moral basis for public affairs.'[1] In October 1915, 48 out of 107 affiliated bodies came from the Labour movement; by 1921 the U.D.C. had 350 affiliated Labour organizations, representing a membership of over a million. These bodies powerfully reinforced the financial support of the few rich backers. But the ideas which they received were more important than the money that they gave. The I.L.P. and other Labour groups were against the war without knowing why. They jumped at the clear answers provided by Morel. Some of his pamphlets came out under the imprint of the I.L.P.; and all its pamphlets on foreign affairs bore the stamp of his inspiration. The Labour party, too, turned to Morel when it began to have doubts about the war. In fact no member of the Labour movement troubled to work out a Socialist foreign policy—if such a thing be possible—so long as Morel was alive. To paraphrase Mrs. Swanwick: Dissent meant the U.D.C.; and the U.D.C. meant E. D. Morel.

[1] H. M. Swanwick, *Builders of Peace*, p. 57.

The Union, as its name implied, was directed primarily against 'secret diplomacy', or perhaps against any diplomacy at all. It echoed Cobden's 'no foreign politics', though with some elaboration. Three out of its four Cardinal Points were negative: no transfer of territory without a plebiscite; no treaty or undertaking without parliamentary sanction; drastic reduction of armaments and nationalization of the arms-traffic. Even the remaining point was mainly negative; a rejection of the Balance of Power. It added, almost as an afterthought: 'the establishment of a Concert of the Powers and the setting up of an International Council whose delibera-tions and decisions shall be public', with treaties of arbitra-tion and Courts 'for their interpretation and enforcement'. This was a long way from the plans for a League of Nations which others were soon to elaborate;[1] and it reflected the practical cast of Morel's mind. The I.L.P. took over these points virtually unaltered, except that 'a federation of the nations' was incongruously dovetailed in along with 'an International Council whose decisions shall be public'.[2]

The U.D.C. was convinced that, if there had been less foreign policy, there would have been no war. Its practical task was therefore to show that there had been nothing in German policy before the war to excite alarm. Morel did this in a penny pamphlet for the I.L.P., *How the War Began*, which came out before the end of 1914, and more elaborately in *Truth and the War*, which sold twenty thousand copies in 1916. Both developed his private verdict: '*you are all guilty—everyone.*' Germany was represented as the aggrieved Power. 'In 1898 Germany began to build a fleet to protect her coast and her commerce.' The conference of Algeciras 'deliberately threw down the gauntlet to Germany'. 'From 1904 [observe the date, it is that of the Anglo-French entente], European policy hatched war as a hen hatches chickens.' Further, 'it is a

[1] Even this half-hearted reference to an international organization was missing from the first private letter which was the prelude to the U.D.C.
[2] In 1916 the U.D.C. added a fifth Point, also negative: universal Free Trade. This, too, was endorsed by the I.L.P.

moral, physical and strategic impossibility to bottle up an elemental force such as that which the German people incarnate. It simply cannot be done.' The Dissenters did not stop with justifying Germany. They treated Austria-Hungary also as a German national state, and therefore claimed that she was fighting a defensive war. Brailsford wrote in *The Nation*: 'Every proposal to take German provinces and dismember Austria is a justification of the German belief that the position of the German race in Central Europe is made tenable only by its vast armies.'[1] Morel said much the same: 'Germany and Austria had the deep-rooted conviction that the national existence was, and is, threatened by a coalition of hostile forces. Nor can I conceive that such a conviction would have survived the sufferings of the war if there was not a substance of fact to buttress it.'[2]

The Dissenters challenged the immediate, as well as the remoter causes of the war. Belgium was, of course, the trickiest point. A few extreme advocates of even-handed justice held that, since every war had two sides, Belgium must be as much at fault in resisting the Germans as they were in invading her. For instance, Vernon Lee, also an early member of the U.D.C., argued that to insist on the neutrality of Belgium was like 'calling for fair play between one man armed with a stick, and threatened by one man (or rather two men!), and a man armed with a long-range rifle'.[3] Bernard Shaw also took this line in a pamphlet called *Common Sense and the War*, a title more than usually impertinent. Shaw argued that Belgian neutrality weakened Germany's strategic position, and was therefore an act of aggression against her. In any case, Belgium had nothing to do with the entry of Great Britain into the war. Grey's policy had been a deliberate trap for Germany, 'the last spring of the old lion'. Having thus destroyed the moral case for the war, Shaw then defended it on strictly practical grounds as a struggle for survival: England must defeat Germany (or Germany defeat

---

[1] *The Nation*, 29 August 1914.   [2] *The Nation*, 28 October 1916.
[3] *The Nation*, 22 August 1914. The sense is clearer than the grammar.

England), and, as Shaw lived in England, he proposed to support the English side of the equation. Shaw enjoyed pricking moral pretensions; he also enjoyed teasing his fellow Dissenters. On the other hand he wished to be secure from the attentions of the police and to be received as an honoured guest at G.H.Q. Supporting the war on immoral grounds satisfied his requirements exactly. Many readers did not understand his intentions. Supporters of the war denounced Shaw, the rigorous Bismarckian, as a pacifist; and Dissenters thought that he had given the game of British morality away. Keir Hardie, for instance, wrote to Shaw: 'Your article will produce an elevation of tone in the national life which will be felt for generations to come. . . . My heart throbs towards you with almost feelings of devotion.'[1]

Most Dissenters shrank from a ruthlessness which rebounded on to their own position. The more usual Dissenting position was to treat Belgium as an innocent victim of rival Imperialist Powers. Brailsford, for instance, wrote: 'So long as we heap up armaments and form diplomatic combinations, in order to win colonies and spheres of influence for ourselves and our friends, so long will the relationship of nations remain on the precarious basis of force.' But he, too, thought that the Belgians had carried things rather far: 'We will not discuss whether the Belgians need have resisted the German invasion. Their courage has been superb; but . . . should we say that a single householder was dishonoured if he did not resist a gang of armed burglars?' In any case, this did not acquit the directors of British policy. A declaration of British support to Belgium, if made before the war, 'would have forced the German General Staff, on the assumption that it consisted of sane men, to reverse their strategical plans. . . . But *the navy was mortgaged to France.*'[2] This last sentence became the Dissenting refrain. Norman Angell said it: 'Belgium had to be sacrificed to the maintenance of the Balance of Power'; so did C. P. Scott: 'No doubt we were

[1] W. Stewart, *Keir Hardie*, p. 359.
[2] H. N. Brailsford, *Belgium and 'the Scrap of Paper'*.

committed to France, Belgium or no Belgium.' Bryce, Morley, Loreburn, Courtney of Penwith, all put their finger on
No. 123 in the Blue Book, where the German Ambassador
was supposed to have offered to trade Belgium in exchange
for British neutrality; and they quoted Gladstone's negotiations of 1870 in order to establish—erroneously in my
opinion—either that a British guarantee to Belgium did not
exist or that there was an obligation on Great Britain to
remain neutral if Belgium was left alone.

The position became easier for the Dissenters when dead-
lock followed the first few weeks of fighting. Instead of
arguing why the war had started, they could discuss how it
should be ended; they could even show how to end it
honourably. The war, in their view, had been caused by the
ententes with France and Russia, not by the German invasion
of Belgium; therefore the Germans would gladly restore
Belgium, the moment that this country repudiated the aggressive designs of its two partners. The Dissenters had some
qualms about leaving north-east France in German occupation; they had no qualms at all about abandoning Russia.
Indeed even those who supported the war hoped that Germany could be somehow defeated without Russia's winning.
Bernard Shaw wrote:

A victory unattainable without Russian aid would be a defeat for
Western European Liberalism. . . . If we cannot without Russian
help beat Potsdam . . . then we shall simply have to 'give Germany
best' and depend upon an alliance with America for our place in
the sun.

—not a bad guess of how things turned out thirty years later.
It was soon an article of faith with the Dissenters that Germany was eager for peace without victory. Pigou, a Fellow
of King's College, Cambridge, asked: why do the allies not
state their peace terms? Is it for fear that the Germans might
accept them?[1] Bertrand Russell answered: 'Probably, even
now, Germany would be willing to evacuate Belgium and

[1] *The Nation,* 6 February 1915.

North-East France, and to come to terms with Russia about the Balkans.'[1]

Clearly the Allies must be harbouring some nefarious design, to refuse such an attractive prospect. And the Dissenters soon discovered what it was: the Allies were prolonging the war so that Russia should gain Constantinople. Charles Trevelyan said in the House of Commons: 'Suppose we knew that Germany would retire from Belgium, and give an indemnity . . . perhaps give back some of Lorraine . . . give Serbia back its independence? What then? Have we got to continue this war until Russia is in possession of Constantinople?'[2] Outhwaite, a Radical from South Africa, almost outdid Urquhart in his obsession about Russia:

> This War is . . . a fight in the main for Russia to obtain possession of Constantinople. If our object is to drive Germany out of France and out of Belgium and compel her to indemnify their people . . . , all that seems to me an object within the capacity of this country which perhaps has been achieved already.[3]

Brailsford pushed this argument to its logical conclusion: if we not merely kept Russia out of Turkey, but gave it to Germany instead, all our troubles would be solved. 'A German Turkey would not be a graver menace to the peace of the world than a British India. The chief menace to the world's liberty is to-day an unsatisfied Germany.' If Germany were given political and economic predominance in Turkey, together with control of the Balkan railways, 'we may hope for a solution of the Alsatian, Serbian, and Polish (and, of course, Belgian) problems, on lines of nationality'.[4]

These ideas reached parliament in November 1915, when Ponsonby and Trevelyan in the Commons, Courtney of Penwith in the Lords, first called for a peace by negotiation—Courtney bravely declaring that he would refuse to *pay* any

---

[1] *The Nation*, 13 February 1915.
[2] 11 October 1916. *Hansard*, fifth series, lxxxvi, 147.
[3] 12 October 1916. *Hansard*, fifth series, lxxxvi, 332–4.
[4] *The Nation*, 1 January 1916. *The Nation* endorsed this solution editorially on 29 July 1916 and 6 January 1917.

indemnity to Germany. The call was repeated in 1916—on 23 February, 24 May, 11 October—and on 12 February 1917. On none of these occasions did the Dissenters divide the House—evidence of their isolation. Their arguments were strictly practical: no discussion of the origins of the war, but solely an insistence that, however it began, it should now be ended by negotiation. On 21 October 1916 the House first heard a constructive alternative, the League of Nations. Lees-Smith, back from the trenches and speaking in uniform, said:

> Security can only be obtained by a scheme by which the nations of Europe and outside agree together that all will guarantee each and each will guarantee all. The purposes of the war will be achieved if there is a League of Nations with an absolute and decisive veto upon any mere aggression, and consideration of any legitimate claims which any of the countries engaged in the War may be able to make good. . . . Go back to the old Liberal tradition and trust yourself boldly to those decent, kindly, humane forces to be found in every man and every nation.[1]

Though the phrase was new to the House of Commons, 'the League of Nations' had become common currency since Lowes Dickinson coined it in August 1914. The phrase was used, the idea supported, by many people who believed that the defeat of Germany should come first, including Sir Edward Grey. Yet it was used more persistently and emphatically by those who regarded the League as a substitute both for the defeat of Germany and for traditional foreign policy. In 1916 three men published detailed schemes for a League of Nations—Hobson, Brailsford, Leonard Woolf. All three were members of the Union of Democratic Control. All three treated the League as synonymous with 'International Government'.

The U.D.C. provided the stage-army which marched forth whenever the League of Nations was discussed. The first scheme for a League, drafted by Leonard Woolf, was commissioned by the Fabian research department. The leading members of this department were Hobson, Lowes Dickinson,

---

[1] *Hansard*, fifth series, lxxxviii, 1728–30.

Richard Cross (solicitor to the Rowntrees), Raymond Unwin, Bernard Shaw. Almost simultaneously another committee worked out a scheme under the chairmanship of Lord Bryce. Its members were Lowes Dickinson, W. H. Dickinson (Liberal M.P.), Hobson, Ponsonby, Graham Wallas, and Richard Cross. Next Lowes Dickinson set up the League of Nations Society; again all its principal members came from the Union of Democratic Control. Yet this did not mean that the League became an essential part of U.D.C. policy. It was rather a fifth wheel, awkwardly tacked on at the end of the argument. Morel himself was significantly absent from every League committee: he had more urgent business. Time and again, the League was spatchcocked in as an afterthought. For instance, the U.D.C. devised peace terms in July 1917. Out of the thirteen points, the League got one half-sentence. It appeared as 'a means of defence which renders old militarism unnecessary'; but obviously the U.D.C. regarded it as of less importance than its old loves—open diplomacy and disarmament. The Labour party provides another instance. In December 1917 it drafted democratic principles of foreign policy (modelled on those of the U.D.C.) for submission to a meeting of Allied Socialists. The draft embraced everything from territorial changes to economic systems. At the last minute a further paragraph was inserted. This begins: 'But it demands, in addition, . . . a Supernational Authority, or League of Nations.'

Bertrand Russell provides an even more striking example. The final chapter of *The Foreign Policy of the Entente* laid down Radical principles of foreign policy: no annexations; renunciation of the right of capture; universal arbitration; no alliances or understandings; 'we shall not engage in war except when we are attacked'. Appended to this is a footnote: 'Unless a League of Great Powers could be formed to resist aggression everywhere. . . . In that case, we might be willing to participate in a war to enforce its decisions.'[1] The contradiction seems startling; but Woodrow Wilson himself did

[1] Bertrand Russell, *Foreign Policy of the Entente*, p. 73.

much the same, when he thought to change the character of the treaty of Versailles by tying the Covenant of the League to its coat-tails. Every advocate of the League weighed with two measures. Their books described at length the misdeeds of statesmen all over the world. Then, in a short final chapter, they assumed that the same statesmen would become persistently virtuous once a League of Nations had been set up.

Moreover the League, like other great phrases in history from the Trinity to the Rights of Man, solved every problem for its votaries while remaining incomprehensible to the detached observer. The members of the U.D.C. believed that it made the defeat of Germany unnecessary. Supporters of the war, such as Gilbert Murray or H. G. Wells, expected it to perpetuate the victory of the Allies. The League would guarantee the security of every country, yet carry through treaty-revision. Pacifists could assert that war solved nothing, yet be confident that a League war would solve everything. The League could cover anything from the Concert of Europe to a system of International Government in which national sovereignty ceased to exist. In 1918 Garvin, the Jingo journalist, thought that a crusade against Bolshevism 'in the decisive sense . . . would be the best way in which the League of Nations could begin and would do more than anything else to confirm belief in its real efficiency and prospects of successful development'.[1] Yet 'a league or concert of nations with an international force' was also advocated by the British Socialist Party, the most revolutionary and pro-Bolshevik group in England, which became the nucleus of the Communist party of Great Britain.

Morel ignored the agitation for a League. Ramsay Mac-Donald did more: he dissented from it. The League, in his own favourite word, was 'quackery'. 'To call national armies an International Police Force seems to me nothing but sticking new misleading labels upon them.'[2] He said much the same in the House of Commons:

[1] J. L Garvin, *Economic Foundations of Peace*, pp. 400–2.
[2] Ramsay MacDonald, *National Defence*, p. 18.

Those who look to guarantees in arms, and military, and force and all that sort of thing, are only just reading once again, in a somewhat different phraseology, but in substance precisely the same, all the chapters that have been written in the history of the world, every one of which has ended in a war.[1]

MacDonald also repudiated the analogy with a police force that had already become popular in League circles: 'My protection really is, not that there is organized force around me, but that there are involuntary social habits around me. . . . It is not so much the policeman that one depends on as public opinion.'[2] MacDonald is often regarded as an empty rhetorician, but he seems in retrospect—despite his style of utterance—the only realist among all the Dissenters. 'The need, therefore, was for disarmament, the end of the prevailing political system of Europe, open diplomacy, and the genuine internationalism of socialism. . . . Then we shall want no League of Nations to Enforce Peace, with its dangers and surrenders to militarism.'[3]

MacDonald's own enthusiasm was for 'open diplomacy', an endless process of talk and discussion; this gave him his hold over the Dissenters. He said of the old diplomacy:

The whole corrupting system should be swept away. It stands like a dirty old slum area, full of vermin and disease, in the midst of a district cleared and improved. . . . Open diplomacy will not remove the *causes* of war; it will enable these causes to dissipate themselves without an explosion. . . . The people and reasonableness will settle them as they arise[4].

And here is his description of the new system, a remarkable proof, incidentally, that his style did not grow on him only in later years:

The days of peace picnics and polite and meaningless speeches are over. They have been empty. Energy that is sleepless and a

[1] *Hansard*, fifth series, 109, 719–22.
[2] *Hansard*, fifth series, 109, 719.
[3] *Labour Leader*, 19 December 1916. This, and other quotations, are from the invaluable book by Van der Slice, *International Labour Diplomacy and Peace 1914–19* (1941).
[4] Ramsay MacDonald, *National Defence*, pp. 115–16.

policy which is pursued from day to day and with complete detail, watching every move in the diplomatic game and with a thoroughly efficient Intelligence Department and Parliamentary policy, are now required if the men who have died for us are not to have died in vain.[1]

It is tempting to go on quoting MacDonald for ever—there is certainly enough material. I cannot resist two further examples. First, his comment on Alsace-Lorraine, a comment which enabled him to avoid any decision between a plebiscite and return to France:

Two races . . . have been thrown into the middle of Europe in this devilish sort of way as though an imp of another region had simply done it in order to make peace impossible. . . . I hope that it is going to be kept as an open door yet.[2]

And his vision of what should happen when the war ended:

We hope . . . that the moment a truce comes . . . the peoples of Europe will come together, and in their enthusiasm and their sorrow and pain and suffering will there and then on the spot, before the experience has gone out of their minds, create something which will make it impossible for such a state of things ever to take place again.[3]

MacDonald only said at greater length what every Dissenter believed: that the peoples of the world had no quarrel with each other and that peace would be secured by democratic government, rather than by the League of Nations.

Discussion of the League has carried me away from my theme. This is historically inevitable. The League was perhaps not an irrelevance; but it was an addition, almost a luxury, and it had little connection with the practical demand for peace terms. 1917 was in every country the great year of discussion for a negotiated peace; it was also the year which saw the dawn of the New World—in more senses than one. The earthly home of this Utopia still stands, as derelict as an abandoned Sandemanian chapel. When next in Soho, push

---

[1] Ramsay MacDonald, *National Defence*, p. 120.
[2] *Hansard*, fifth series, xcviii, 2034.
[3] *Hansard*, fifth series, 107, 588.

your way through the parked cars and the equally stationary, though more aged, whores; brave the mixed smell of Continental cooking and exotic barber shops; and stand reverently before No. 5 Gerrard Street. There above a bakery was the 1917 Club, home of idealist enthusiasm: founded to commemorate the great year of liberty, and perishing appropriately in 1931, when J. A. Hobson, withdrawing in protest against the confusion of the accounts, fell heavily downstairs.

Two great events caused this Dawn. One was the entry of the United States into the war; the other was the Russian Revolution. Together they determined the shape of the world in which we still live. Both marked the triumph of idealism. The war to make the world safe for democracy eclipsed the conflict of rival Imperialisms. At the beginning the Russian Revolution counted for more with the Dissenters. A democratic Russia was 'the virtual solution of the problem of the war'[1]—the problem, that is, how Germany could be defeated without Russia's winning. Snowden said: 'It has given us a new hope in democracy and revived our faith in Internationalism.'[2] Not that it converted the Dissenters to support of the war. On the contrary it made them more convinced than ever that the war was unnecessary. They had long regarded old Russia's claim to Constantinople as the one obstacle to peace. New Russia had dropped this claim. The Radicals still believed that Germany was prepared to withdraw from Belgium and north-eastern France. Soon they heard rumours of the Austrian peace offer, supposedly made in April 1917. Russia, Germany, Austria-Hungary all wanted peace. Yet it was not made. Why? The fault could only lie with the governments of England and France. France received most of the blame now that tsarist Russia was out of the way. The suspicions of Agadir were revived; and France appeared as an Imperialist Power, fighting for the left bank of the Rhine, with which Alsace-Lorraine was easily confused. But the British government did not escape condemnation. *The Nation* regarded the British demands for Mesopotamia and the German colonies as

[1] *The Nation*, 24 March 1917.   [2] *Hansard*, fifth series, xciii, 1625.

the principal obstacle to peace.[1] Ponsonby told the House of Commons that the British government had 'prostituted the original disinterested motives with which you entered the war and . . . substituted a mean craving for gain and an arrogant demand for Imperial aggrandisement and domination, without the consent of the people, and behind the backs of the people'.[2]

In the course of 1917 the Dissenters discovered a more dramatic explanation. It was the proposal to 'dismember' Austria-Hungary which was prolonging the war. This became the principal charge against the Never-Endians, as The Nation called them. As late as July 1918 The Nation asserted that the aim of dismembering Austria-Hungary would prolong the war for years; and even when the prophecy turned out to be false the advocates of national states were accused of having been willing to prolong the war if this had been necessary. The creation of national states was also condemned as wrong in itself—wrong in principle, doubly wrong as making reconciliation with Germany impossible. Some Radicals said that the nationalities should be content with the Home Rule which had been granted to Ireland—though the Irish were not; most Radicals did not go even that far.

Their opinions are worth quoting; they had curious echoes twenty years later. Ponsonby said of the Czecho-Slovacs (sic): 'Very few people, I find, have the remotest idea who they are.'[3] Outhwaite detected in them another aspect of the Slav menace: 'Probably 999 out of 100,000 of our people had never heard of Czecho-Slovak. I believe there is no such people as Czecho-Slovak.'[4] Massingham wrote in The Nation: 'The idea of an independent Tchecho-Slovakia rested on the support of Russian imperialism. . . . No section of opinion here either vetoes or disapproves a closer approach to Austria.'[5] Later, Czecho-Slovakia became 'a bad solution of

[1] The Nation, 30 June 1917.
[2] 19 December 1917. Hansard, fifth series, xciii, 1999.
[3] Hansard, fifth series, xc, 1178. 20 February 1917.
[4] Hansard, fifth series, xc, 1298.   [5] The Nation, 12 May 1917.

the European question . . . chauvinistic. . . . It is pure nationalism . . . the latest scheme for the re-partition of Europe,
designed to aggrandize one racial stock—a very fine one—at
the expense of another. We like Moloch no better when his
votaries dance to a Slav measure than to a Teutonic one.'[1]
The Nation was also fierce against Poland: 'A great scheme
of annexation at Germany's and Austria's expense. . . . War,
famine, plague and their attendant demons of hate and lust,
threaten to devour the societies of men. And the statesmen
offer them a brand-new Poland!'[2] The condemnation was repeated still more strongly after the armistice: 'Strassburg
(*sic*) and Posen may go; the blow will be endured and a
League may be created. Take Danzig and German Bohemia,
and no League of Nations can possibly be created.'[3]

This new current of argument brought back into events
men who had been silent since the outbreak of war. Philip
Morrell, one-time paymaster of the Foreign Policy Committee, said of the dismemberment of the Austrian empire:
'nothing which seems to me more impolitic, more foolish,
more mad.'[4] The most important figure to step forward
again was Noel Buxton, the man who had taken the lead after
Agadir and whose moderation carried great weight. For
many years he had championed the cause of Bulgaria; and at
the beginning of the war attempted to win her as an ally by
an offer of the Macedonian territory that had fallen to Serbia.
Now he abandoned the national principle. Since Bulgaria
could not have Macedonia, no other nation should be allowed
anything, Serbia least of all. His earlier advocacy of a Jugo-
Slav federation, he said, 'had depended absolutely on the
feasibility of restoring to their rightful owners the non-
Serbian and non-Roumanian lands of the south'. The national
states, once so admired, now appeared to him as 'a congeries
of small states . . . not an attractive proposition'. They were
merely a device for extending French hegemony: 'Heaven

[1] *The Nation*, 6 July, 26 October, 7 September 1918.
[2] *The Nation*, 15 June 1918.   [3] *The Nation*, 18 January 1919.
[4] 16 May 1917. *Hansard*, fifth series, xciii, 1694.

help us, if the only security in the future is to be reliance on strategical military forces of that kind.'[1] As for the French claim to Alsace-Lorraine, this was simply a trick to lay hands on 'the minerals' of Lorraine.[2]

Opposition to the war recovered its moral force. Before 1917 the Dissenters, pure pacifists apart, had been sane and rational, but they had been battling against the moral current. The Russian revolution, the Austrian peace offer, and finally the publication by the Bolsheviks of the so-called secret treaties, branded the supporters of the war as cynical and imperialist. Even Wilson's Fourteen Points did not restore the moral superiority of the war-makers; for the British and still more the French government were accused of planning to evade them—an accusation which swelled during the actual peace-making later. During 1917 the Dissenters repeatedly divided the House—a striking sign that they had recovered confidence. Thirty-two voted in favour of the Russian peace terms on 16 May; 19 in favour of the Reichstag peace resolution on 26 July; 18 in favour of the Stockholm conference on 16 August; and 28 for a declaration of war aims on 13 February 1918. The figures are not impressive—always less than the support which Fox and Charles Grey received during the war against revolutionary France. But they were an immense improvement on the four or six who had raised their voices in the first two years. All the same, the Dissenters were embarked on a strange course. These votes were cast in support of what Noel Buxton called 'an anti-annexationist and restoration settlement',[3] in other words a return to the *status quo* of 1914. Radicals of an earlier age would have been amazed to see their twentieth-century descendants marching under the banner of the Restoration and insisting that in international affairs, as in everything

[1] 24 July 1917. *Hansard*, fifth series, xcviii, 1177.
[2] 30 July 1917. *Hansard*, fifth series, xcviii, 836. It is tiresome for this theory that there are no minerals in Alsace, about which the French felt just as strongly.
[3] 19 December 1917. *Hansard*, fifth series, c, 2040.

else, the best thing was to stand still, or rather to go back. The Radical Utopia now lay in the past, not in the future.

The movement for a peace of restoration reached its climax with the appeal for peace made in November 1917 by Lord Lansdowne—grandson of the Lord Henry Petty who had won Fox's admiration by demanding the liberation of Europe in 1806. Lansdowne was an extreme Conservative. To his bewilderment he was taken up by the Radicals. He found himself in the company of Noel Buxton, F. W. Hirst, Massingham of *The Nation*, and the business men from Liverpool who had once backed E. D. Morel's campaign over the Congo. These men formed the Lansdowne Committee for a peace by negotiation; their agitation flourished until the decisive victory of the Allies in the late summer of 1918. It was a strange end for the middle-class Radicals that they should rally under the leadership of a man who had broken with Gladstone over the Irish Land Act of 1881, had forced the crisis over the House of Lords by his uncompromising opposition to Liberal legislation, and now came hotfoot from wrecking the last chance of settling the Irish question by consent. The 'weird combination'[1] went further. Lord Milner, sometimes called the second figure in the War Cabinet, also favoured 'a peace of adjustment', and approached the Webbs through Haldane, in hope of securing the support of the Labour party. Milner's 'adjustment' was that Germany should be allowed a free hand in Eastern Europe, on condition she surrendered her conquests in the West; the treaty of Brest-Litovsk was to be the foundation for a partnership to protect Western civilization against Bolshevism.

Once upon a time the Labour party would have been delighted to co-operate with Germany against Russia. With the fall of tsardom that time had passed. Milner's overture met with no response. Moreover it had come too late. The Labour party was at last beginning to devise its own foreign policy for 'the democracy'; it no longer needed guidance from Lord

[1] Wedgwood, 16 May 1918. *Hansard*, fifth series, 106, 610.

Milner or anybody else. The process had taken a long time. In 1914 the Labour party supported the war almost unanimously. The Dissenters of the I.L.P. were forced into alliance with the few remaining Radicals, and away from the trade union leaders. When Allied Socialists met in February 1915, the Labour party agreed without discussion that, while capitalism caused wars, this particular war had been caused by the German invasion of Belgium and France. There was another striking breach with the pre-war Dissenting outlook on Keir Hardie's death in September 1915. The electoral truce was broken at Merthyr, his constituency; and a bellicose follower of Hyndman defeated the official Labour candidate, who had been nominated by the I.L.P. Most Labour leaders welcomed this ostensible defeat for their own party. In 1916 the party conference, the first since the outbreak of war, supported the war without a division. MacDonald, explaining that he was an opponent of secret diplomacy, not a friend of Germany, lamented: 'Oh how sad it was, how heart-breaking it was, that some of them had to stand up and face the Conference with pride in their hearts as to what it was and doubt in their hearts as to what it would be!'

The Labour party was pushed into independence, willy-nilly, by the changed political circumstances which followed Lloyd George's seizure of power at the end of 1916. Asquith's government had been parliamentary even when it became a coalition; and since there were few Labour M.P.s, the party had little influence on policy. Lloyd George's government was made outside parliament, or even against it; for Asquith still commanded a powerful majority at the moment of his fall. Lloyd George owed his position to 'public opinion', which in this case meant newspaper proprietors from Riddell and Northcliffe to C. P. Scott. He was more popular in the country than in parliament, which he rarely attended; and he defined his policy in public speeches, not in the House of Commons. He dealt directly with the great 'interests', not with parliamentary votes; and the greatest of these interests was 'Labour'. Henderson secured a seat in the War Cabinet as the voice of this interest, not as leader of the few Labour M.P.s. Moreover Lloyd George endorsed the view that Labour spoke for 'the people' and that they, as the old Radicals held, were peculiarly pacific and enlightened. He told the Labour party executive: 'It seemed inconceivable that any Minister should make terms of Peace without consulting representatives of Labour'; and he hoped for, or perhaps promised, Labour representation at the peace conference: 'I think nothing could conduce more to getting a satisfactory peace . . . because you want above everything else to ensure that there will be no more wars in the future.'[1] Here was a clear invitation to the Labour party to formulate its own foreign policy.

A second, and more powerful, impulse came with the first Russian revolution. Democratic Russia denounced the secret treaties and called for a peace with 'no annexations and no indemnities'. This was a challenge to Socialist parties in other Allied countries. It seemed at first as though the only response would come from the extreme Left. In June 1917 the I.L.P. and the B.S.P. set up the United Socialist Council —the first appearance of the Popular Front, though by no means the last; and this body summoned a Convention at Leeds, the name recalling the Chartist Convention of 1839 or even the Convention of the great French Revolution. The Leeds Convention was intended to inaugurate the British revolution. Its chief resolution, supported by MacDonald and Snowden among others, called for the setting up of Workers' and Soldiers' Councils—Soviets in fact. The Convention also

---

[1] MacDonald published his shorthand note of Lloyd George's statement in *The Times* of 15 November 1918. According to this, Lloyd George said: 'It is such a long way off, peace. I sincerely hope myself that there will be a Labour representative at this conference and I think etc.' MacDonald however interpreted this as a definite pledge for representation, whatever the Labour party's position after the war ended: 'Mr. Lloyd George pledged himself to the Labour Party at the War Office that if it joined his Government there and then for the purpose of the war Labour would be represented at the Peace Conference.' (*Forward*, 16 November 1918.) Lloyd George won the competition in imprecision, and Labour had to make do with G. N. Barnes.

endorsed the Russian peace programme and instructed the British government to do the same. A historic moment. Previously British Radicals had railed against alliance with Russia. Henceforth advanced Dissenters defined their foreign policy as endorsement of whatever Russia happened to be doing at the moment. This was the only achievement at Leeds. The eleven hundred delegates dispersed. The Convention vanished into limbo, taking the United Socialist Council along with it.

Nevertheless Henderson did not ignore the warning that Labour feeling was moving towards independence. He moved with it. The occasion for his break to freedom was the proposed Socialist conference at Stockholm, where Allied representatives would meet Germans for the first time since the outbreak of war. Henderson at first opposed the conference, then swung round in order to strengthen the flagging belligerence of the Russian people; or, as he put it, 'using the political weapon to supplement our military activities'. He was in an odd position—at once a member of the War Cabinet and leader of the most important Labour movement on the Allied side. He found no conflict in this. He could be the Rt. Hon. Arthur Henderson one day, and close associate the next of such trade union leaders as Robert Williams, who told a party conference: 'I say, praise God when there will be a notice "to let" outside Buckingham Palace!' Henderson was happiest in double harness. We always think of him as one of a pair. Webb and Henderson devised the constitution for the Labour party in 1918; MacDonald and Henderson were denounced by Lenin as the two Socialist lackeys of Imperialism; J. H. Thomas replied 'Me or 'Enderson' when asked who would be the first Labour Prime Minister; Lansbury and Henderson saved the soul of the Labour party in 1931. So now, in 1917, Henderson thought that he could work with Lloyd George to win the war, and with the Dissenters to win the peace.

The War Cabinet did not stomach this arrangement. When Henderson went over to support of the Stockholm conference, he found himself 'on the mat' and was forced to resign. 'I refused to do what I never will do, namely, desert the people who sent me into the government.' He did not go into opposition. Though he resolved never again to join a government where Labour was not in a majority, he successfully resisted a proposal that the remaining Labour ministers should withdraw, on the ground that it would embarrass the government in its prosecution of the war. But his own path was fixed: though not in opposition, he was independent and intended to remain so. The Labour delegates were prevented from going to Stockholm; nevertheless the Labour movement, under Henderson's guidance, set out to create its own foreign policy. Thus resolved, where could it turn for ideas? Only to the U.D.C. The Union had staked its claim to provide an alternative foreign policy. Now it struck gold.

MacDonald was the most important link. His influence obviously increased when the Labour party drifted towards independence. His hand can be seen in the phrase in the party programme against 'the old entanglements and mystifications of Secret Diplomacy and the formation of Leagues against Leagues'. But all the intellectuals of the U.D.C. streamed into the Labour party, packing its Advisory Committee on International Questions—a sort of rival foreign office. Only Morel himself was absent. He was too independent to work under the guidance of others; and in any case was out of the way at this moment, sent to prison on the most forced charge ever trumped up against a critic even by the British government.[1] Not that the Labour party limited itself to the U.D.C. The Advisory Committee also contained members who supported the war—Toynbee, Hammond, J. L. Stocks, on one occasion a memorandum from Namier; and

[1] Morel sent a copy of *Truth and the War* to Romain Rolland who, he thought, was in France, but was actually in Switzerland. It was an offence to send printed matter to a neutral, though not to an allied, country; and on this thin charge Morel was sentenced to six months' hard labour. It is a wonder that the government did not manufacture evidence against his sexual morality.

future Communists—Palme Dutt and Saklatvala. But the U.D.C. set the tone for them all.

The outcome was a statement of war aims, issued by the Labour party and the T.U.C. on 28 December 1917. Apart from a few changes of phrase, it was indistinguishable from proposals which the U.D.C. had made in July. There was the same repudiation of the old diplomacy, the same refusal to discriminate between enemies and allies, the same emphasis on reconciliation with Germany. But soon the Labour movement ran into a characteristic tangle. Henderson still wanted international action despite the failure of Stockholm. In February 1918 the T.U.C. and the Labour party organized an Inter-Allied Labour and Socialist conference—thus excluding the I.L.P. and the B.S.P. who would have had to be invited if the meeting had been called by the International Socialist Bureau. The conference turned the December statement upside down, largely under French prompting. The League of Nations was placed at the beginning, instead of appearing as a grudging addition, and military sanctions were added to it; Poland received special and mandatory recognition 'with free access to the sea'; and a clause was put in, recognizing 'the claims to independence made by the Czecho-Slovaks and the Yugo-Slavs'. All this was in flagrant contradiction with the policy of the U.D.C. It caused endless confusion that the Labour party, true to Henderson's spirit, never decided between the two outlooks. It pursued both at once: approving the national claims to independence and sympathizing with the German grievances which these claims caused; demanding Poland's access to the sea and denouncing 'the Corridor'; preaching pacifism and sanctions, disarmament and security. This is tiresome for those who want men and events to fall into a simple pattern, but this is how it was. If the Labour men were full of contradictions, so were their Radical predecessors; and so, for that matter, is everyone else.

Few noticed the contradiction at the time. The Labour party had spoken on foreign policy with one voice abroad and another at home even in Keir Hardie's days; and the habit was never lost. Now the declaration of Allied Socialists was clearly marked For Export; Labour policy continued to be found in the statement of December 1917 so far as the British public was concerned. This statement was to achieve a remarkable success. The government had hitherto evaded all demands for a definition of British war aims; and no doubt Lloyd George would have held out longer if parliament alone had been concerned. But he was anxious to keep the Labour movement in a good temper. On 5 January 1918 he called a meeting of trade union leaders and informed them that the government's policy was identical with that of the Labour statement, if in slightly different words. This was certainly a staggering achievement: the U.D.C. was dictating foreign policy, through the agency of the Labour movement, when E. D. Morel was still in gaol. It hardly seemed necessary to have a Bolshevik revolution in England when the Prime Minister, ignoring parliament, announced his policy by saying 'ditto' to Henderson and MacDonald at a Labour meeting.[1] The Soviets had already arrived. The impression was no doubt misleading. Lloyd George was an opportunist— that is why Lenin admired him. He was concerned at the moment to get men freed for the Army; and if a demagogic, even a Dissenting, speech to trade union leaders made this easier, he did not worry about the constitutional implications nor about the difficulties that it might create for him in the future. No doubt the Labour leaders were not as much taken in as Lloyd George imagined. Still, they were not alone in dreaming that he might revert to his pre-war attitude of Dissent once the war was won—and so he did, though too late for it to be of any use to him or anyone else.

In any case, the Labour leaders placed a stronger hope in Woodrow Wilson, whom they supposed to be that impossible thing—a Dissenter in power; and maybe he came as

---

[1] Of course Lloyd George made out that Labour was saying 'ditto' to him. 'Their proposals did not differ in any material respect from those which we were putting forward.' (*War Memoirs*, v, 2485.) But the dates are against him.

near it as any man has ever done. The Dissenters, and not they alone, were misled by their dealings with Colonel House, Wilson's personal representative. He, when in England, saw men of every shade of opinion. He went from Lloyd George to Henderson, from Northcliffe to MacDonald; he talked with Lansbury and would no doubt have met Guy Aldred or John Maclean if he had known of their existence. Each received the impression of being House's especial favourite. Englishmen never realized that even the most friendly Americans, including Wilson and House, looked on all Europeans as aboriginal savages—a mistake repeated by Winston Churchill in regard to F. D. Roosevelt and Harry Hopkins during the second World war. American statesmen might like some Europeans more than others and even detect quaint resemblances to their own outlook; but they no more committed themselves to a particular group or country than a nineteenth-century missionary committed himself to the African tribe in which he happened to find himself. One set of savages might be a bit better than another; but all needed saving by the superior enlightenment of the New World. The Dissenters did not grasp this. They even supposed that they were flattering Wilson by their approval. The T.U.C. sent him their official blessing: 'Your ideals are those of British Labour. British Labour gives you its earnest and united support.' Lansbury's *Herald*, which was pretty far to the Left, wrote on 1 February 1919: 'Wilson is winning because he has to a certain extent identified himself with the common people.'

The general election of December 1918 encouraged the Dissenting tendency to put all their money on Wilson. Though most Labour candidates demanded reparations and the punishment of war-criminals as well as a peace that would make the world safe for democracy and though Coalition candidates were theoretically committed to the League of Nations and the Fourteen Points as well as to a punitive peace, the result seemed to be a victory for 'reaction'. Henceforth Lloyd George was, at best, the prisoner of his associates. For these the Dissenters had a rigid distrust. The old I.L.P. stalwart, Fred Jowett, wrote of Lord Robert Cecil, then championing the League:

> Lord Robert is boosted in the press as though he were the friend of man, but in reality he is probably one of the most deadly enemies of the common people to be found elsewhere than among Russian Grand Dukes and German Junkers.[1]

And when Sir Eric Drummond was appointed Secretary-General of the League, MacDonald commented:

> He has been brought up in the ways of the Foreign Office, trained in the methods of discredited diplomacy, with no Democratic vision and no conception of what World Democracy means, and it is beyond reason to expect from him any inspiration which would make the League anything more than it is now—the organ of the victors to dominate the world.[2]

The Dissenters did not admit for one moment that, in voting for the Coalition, the people had deserted them, or that they had ceased to be 'the voice of the people'. They simply concluded that they must make their voice heard in some other way. When peace-making started, the Labour leaders planned to call an anti-conference of their own, which would lay down the terms of 'a people's peace', regardless of what the official statesmen were doing. An International Socialist meeting was in fact held at Berne from 26 January to 10 February 1919, when Germans met some Allied Socialists for the first time.

The Berne conference was not a success. The most important leaders were too busy to come—wrestling with demobilization and re-employment or, in Germany, suppressing the extreme Socialists. Dissent miscarried on an international scale. All the more urgent therefore to press it at home. The Dissenters were primed to attack the peace settlement long before anything emerged at Paris. Early in April there appeared the draft of the League Covenant. The Labour men projected a meeting in London to discuss, and still more to amend, it. Still deluded about their American backers, they

---

[1] The Bradford *Pioneer*, 21 February 1919.
[2] *Forward*, 24 May 1919.

invited House to attend the meeting. He refused; and the Labour Dissenters realized that he was not their ally after all. They ceased to believe that Wilson would achieve anything for them. Henceforward he became a broken reed, 'bamboozled' in Keynes's phrase; or, as MacDonald wrote at the time, 'the American was no match for European diplomatists'. Encouragement came to the Dissenters, however, from an unexpected quarter: Lloyd George. He had just devised a tactic which he was to practise with varying success in the following years. Being the prisoner of the 'reactionaries', he would give his gaolers rope enough to hang themselves. He went along with their wild schemes until public opinion in England turned round; then he appeared as the Radical champion—tardy but victorious. The tactic worked over intervention in Russia; it worked to some extent in regard to the treaty of Versailles; unfortunately a noose of the Irish rope got tangled round Lloyd George's own neck, and he could not shake off the Black-and-Tans to the end of his days.

In May 1919 Lloyd George tried out his tactic for the first time. He crammed the draft treaty with all the fierce proposals which the British people had favoured during the general election. Germany was to pay vast undefined reparations, to disarm completely, and to be excluded from the League; she lost all her colonies and was to surrender Danzig and much of Silesia to the Poles. Then Lloyd George waited for public opinion to explode; or rather he himself waved a lighted match in the hope of finding gunpowder. Not only did he expostulate with his colleagues at the peace conference. He sent for Vandervelde, until recently president of the Socialist International,[1] and urged him to whip up Socialist feeling against the peace terms.[2] This was Dissent of an unusual kind: a British Prime Minister intriguing with International Socialism against his colleagues, his political supporters, his

[1] He had resigned when the Belgian Socialists refused to meet the Germans at Berne, a meeting which he himself favoured.
[2] Vandervelde told the story to Mr. Van der Slice in 1937. Van der Slice, *International Labour Diplomacy and Peace*, p. 372.

Allies, and his own policy. Was Vandervelde the only one to be prompted by Lloyd George? It seems unlikely. Henderson and MacDonald often breakfasted with Lloyd George in Paris. They must have known something of what was in his mind. It is at any rate a tempting conjecture that both of them, and perhaps the Treasury official J. M. Keynes as well, acted on Lloyd George's suggestion when they denounced the proposed terms of peace.

The draft terms were published early in May. The Labour party condemned them with hardly a day's delay. This time the Labour party got in ahead of the U.D.C. Its statement was issued on 8 May; that of the U.D.C. only on 9 May. But the two were in exactly the same terms. The hand might be that of Henderson; the voice was the voice of E. D. Morel. It was wrong to deprive Germany of her colonies, since war was 'in part the product of frustrated colonial ambitions'. Reparations were wrong: the Germans would become 'a people of serfs working for their conquerors in arms'. The concealed annexation of the Saar was 'a violation of the principle of self-determination'. Poland 'cannot but prove a centre of bitter racial conflict in Europe'; by her frontiers 'violence is done to the right of the people to determine their national allegiance'. Silesia in particular was 'a really astounding act of robbery'. Morel summed up the verdict with his usual sharpness a little later: 'If this Treaty stands, your League of Nations . . . will be the most powerful engine of oppression the world has ever seen.'

The Labour party, the U.D.C., and Lloyd George had to wait longer for the harvest than seemed likely in the golden days of May 1919. It would be many years before public opinion exploded effectively against the peace settlement of Versailles; and the result of the explosion would then be unwelcome to those who had first tried to set it off. What was important at the time was that the Labour party had asserted itself as the party of Dissent. Once without a foreign policy of its own, and then almost unanimous in support of the war, it had gradually drifted into a position identical with that of the Dissenters in the U.D.C. Henceforward it rejected official policy root and branch. The Establishment favoured Versailles; Dissent opposed it, and Dissent meant predominantly the Labour party. To put things even more crudely, the Establishment was pro-French, and Dissent pro-German.

Not pro-Russian? This is another, and essential, part of the story. The first Russian revolution—the democratic revolution of March 1917—had seemed to solve the Dissenting dilemma. New Russia wished to make a peace without annexations or indemnities; it ceased to be a danger to Germany. Therefore the Dissenters no longer needed to choose between the two; they could be friendly to both. The Bolshevik revolution of November estranged all but the most extreme Socialists in England. The Labour party conference at Nottingham early in 1918 welcomed the exiled Kerensky much more warmly than it did Litvinov, Lenin's representative. It was not only that the Bolsheviks dropped selfishly out of the war. The democratic Socialist leaders of the West became the principal targets for Lenin's abuse—Henderson and MacDonald above all. Once the Kaiser was overthrown, the British Labour movement again chose Germany as against Bolshevik Russia. Its policy of conciliation—whether at the Berne meeting or in the attacks on the peace treaty—was in part designed to save Germany for Western democracy and to build her up as a barrier against Bolshevism.

This choice threatened Labour with unwelcome allies. It had no objection to the German Social Democrats; indeed found in these its closest spiritual kin once the passions of war began to subside. But anti-Bolshevism forced Labour towards the most aggressive and reactionary members of the British government. Labour believed that democracy was the best answer to Bolshevism; Churchill, Curzon and others wanted a war of intervention to restore tsardom. Intervention may have started in 1918 as a move against the Germans, though even that is doubtful—the most effective weapon against the Germans would have been to co-operate with Trotsky. By 1919 this argument lost any force it once

L

had. It makes one despair of the honesty of historians that the myth should still be accepted or even considered. Churchill, secretary of state for war, made no secret of his object. 'There is a Russia somewhere, and not far away if only it could be evolved, which represents and embodies all that treasury of the centuries which the nation has built up from the days of Peter the Great. . . . Well did we know it in the early days of the War.'[1] He was warmly seconded by Sir Samuel Hoare, later a leading apostle of non-intervention in Spain: 'A policy of no-intervention is in principle a negation of everything that the League of Nations stands for. If the League is to develop it will have to take sides. . . . I do not believe that a policy of no-intervention is possible.'[2] The Bolsheviks and their opponents had much in common: both followed a policy calculated to bring out the worst in the other side. With Lenin this was perhaps deliberate: he wanted to show that 'the imperialist bandits' had no redeeming feature. But it is difficult to understand how democratic statesmen could rejoice at forcing the Bolsheviks on to a course of terror and dictatorship. Lloyd George, as usual, saw more clearly; but again as usual, paid out the rope to his wild associates.

The Labour movement opposed intervention more from dislike of further war than from any love of the Bolsheviks. And even this opposition took some time to warm up. A resolution at the party conference in June 1919 demanded 'direct action'—the phrase of the time for a general strike—against intervention in Russia. The few Labour M.P.s hurried to defend the constitution. Clynes denounced 'this blow to democracy', and asked: 'Did this mean that any class which could exercise the power should have the right to terrorize a Labour government?' Smillie, the Miners' President, answered him with an echo of the old Dissenting hostility to established institutions: 'If they believed that the Government deceived and lied to the people in order to get returned,

[1] 5 November 1919. *Hansard*, fifth series, cxx, 1631.
[2] 5 November 1919. *Hansard*, fifth series, cxx, 1582.

if that was true, was the great Labour Movement not to take
any action to get rid of a Government that was sitting there
through fraud and deceit?' Herbert Morrison called the report of the parliamentary party 'an insult to the energy, the
intelligence and the vigour of the whole Labour Movement
of the country'. However, the conference decided that only
the trade unions could resolve on direct action; and they did
nothing.

Perhaps nothing would ever have been done, if intervention had been limited to support of the Denikins and Kol-
chaks, the Yudenichs and Wrangels. In the spring of 1920
British backing of Poland touched off a real resistance. Poland
was not merely an enemy of Bolshevism; she was, far more,
the worst blot on the settlement of Versailles. The friends of
Germany and the friends of Russia combined against her.
Tom Shaw, who was himself to be secretary of state for war,
said at the annual conference in June 1920: 'Potsdam and
Berlin in their heyday of military power never approached the
streets of Warsaw, where sabres and brilliant military uniform were the order of the day'—evidence, as the future
showed, of Polish romanticism, not of military efficiency. On
10 May London dockers refused to load munitions for Poland
on to the *Jolly George*. This was the signal for action. The
Labour moderates were driven forward whether they would
or no. The Advisory Committee commented: 'the official
representatives of Labour would be quite unable to disregard
the feeling among the workers or to oppose it even if they
desired to do so.' The Committee added: 'The refusal of the
workers to make war on the Soviet government does not
imply that they necessarily approve the principles upon which
that government is based, still less everything which it is
reported to have done.' This reluctance to be identified with
the Bolsheviks appeared throughout the crisis. The joint
executives of the T.U.C. and Labour party merely said: 'Such
a war would be an intolerable crime against humanity.' The
Special Conference which resolved on direct action did so
'(i) to resist any and every form of military and naval

intervention against the Soviet Government of Russia'; and '(ii) also in order to sweep away secret bargaining and diplomacy'. The U.D.C. got its word in; but there was not a hint that Russia was a Socialist country or 'the Workers' State'.

The Councils of Action which were set up in August 1920 marked the nearest point to revolution ever reached in this country. The Dissenters went beyond opposition and imposed an alternative foreign policy of their own. Even members of parliament supported the threat of revolution. Clynes, the outstanding member of the Labour party in the House of Commons, said: 'No Parliamentary or political measures, we felt, could be effective in themselves.' J. H. Thomas, president of the T.U.C., added: 'If this resolution is to be given effect to, it means a challenge to the whole Constitution of the country (Cheers).' A. G. Cameron, chairman of the Labour Executive, swelled the chorus: 'If the powers that be endeavour to interfere too much, we may be compelled to do things that will cause them to abdicate.' These high-sounding words proved unnecessary. Lloyd George was delighted to turn the storm against his unruly colleagues, and assured the Councils of Action that they were knocking at an open door. With similar opportunism, he disregarded the official machinery of diplomacy; and Ernest Bevin became, 'at the express wish of the Prime Minister', the agent of negotiation between Russia and the British government—his first experience of diplomacy, though unfortunately not his last. The danger of war vanished overnight, assisted no doubt by the fact that the Poles managed to win without British aid. A fortnight later Lloyd George went to the south of France; and Balfour, as acting Prime Minister, attempted to restore the constitutional proprieties by insisting that a Labour delegation to him be composed solely of M.P.s. The Labour movement still acted as an independent power, and nominated Adamson and Purcell as 'accredited representatives' to the peace conference between Russia and Poland at Riga. The British government refused

to issue passports for them; and Labour acquiesced. It was
not worth while insisting once the conflict had been won.

Still, the turmoil which began with the attack on the peace
settlement and ended with the Councils of Action left an
enduring impression. Labour might believe in 'the inevita-
bility of gradualness' at home; it was revolutionary in its
foreign policy, or thought it was. Versailles had taught it that
the governing class was irredeemably wicked; the Councils
of Action had shown that this wickedness could be arrested
before it passed into action. Labour relied on 'direct action'
until it won political power; then it would sweep away the
existing evils by 'open diplomacy'. E. D. Morel stood
triumphant. The Union of Democratic Control and the
Labour movement were one so far as foreign policy was
concerned.

Let me give two illustrations of this marriage, one from
each side. C. P. Trevelyan was a founder of the U.D.C. He
bore an honoured Liberal name, had been a Radical M.P.
before the war, and an advocate of a negotiated peace during
it. In 1919 he joined the Labour party. He explained his conversion in *From Liberalism to Labour* (1920). Before 1914,
he argued, a Radical could do more for social reform as a
Liberal than in the Labour party. But there had been three
decisive Liberal failures. Failure before the war to prevent
secret diplomacy: parliament never discovered 'why Germany should be particularly selected as an enemy or Russia
. . . . as a friend'. Failure during the war to prevent the secret
treaties: from their publication 'dates the change in the attitude of British Labour'—and his own conversion. Failure
after the war to prevent the peace settlement and especially
its crimes against self-determination: Germans had been
annexed to Poland, Austrians to Italy and Czecho-Slovakia,
Serbs and Hungarians to Roumania, Bulgarians to Serbia, a
compendious list. The basis of Labour foreign policy would be
friendship with Russia. 'Britain and Russia will be the great
common international force.' Together they would overthrow the system of Versailles, liberate Germany, and defeat

the French Jingoes. Though Trevelyan later became an extreme Socialist, there was not a word in his confession of faith about nationalization or the capital levy. Foreign affairs alone had carried him into the Labour party.

And now the illustration on the other side. On armistice day 1920, the U.D.C. held a meeting exclusively for ex-servicemen at the Kingsway Hall. The Mayor of Stepney, a Labour man who had fought in the war, took the chair. He said: 'The U.D.C. told us we were deceived. They were right and we were wrong. . . . When I was in the army I used to take occasion to chat with the men and with the officers, particularly with the men, and I have often asked the men what they went to fight for. I always got the same answer: they were fighting for something far bigger than the question of a King or Country. They believed, and we believed, that they were fighting for the good of the whole world. That is where the government betrayal comes in.'[1] The same Mayor of Stepney said a little later at the Labour party conference: 'So long as they had capitalist governments they could not trust them with armaments.' Arthur Henderson called this view 'absolutely absurd and futile'.[2] The Mayor of Stepney was Major C. R. Attlee.

[1] Swanwick, *Builders of Peace*, p. 60.
[2] Henderson continued: 'they could not afford to ignore this question of defence.' The country that Henderson wanted defence against, was France.

VI

BETWEEN THE WARS

THE SEARCH FOR A POLICY

AT first glance controversy on foreign policy between the wars falls into a simple pattern. The Labour and Liberal parties, usually in opposition, supported collective security and the League of Nations. The Conservative or National government, as it was later called, relied on traditional diplomacy and regarded the League, at best, as an additional channel for negotiations. This is now more or less the official Labour version of the past. It is hardly nearer the truth than the Conservative defence that they would have made the country secure by great armaments if only the 'idealists' had left them alone. To judge by what Conservatives say nowadays, no one would guess that they were in power with large majorities for seventeen out of the twenty years between the wars. They could have done what they liked if only they had known what to do, and therefore must bear most of the responsibility for the mistakes which led to the war of 1939. Their best excuse is that they were carrying out a Dissenting foreign policy twenty years too late, and that their most wrongheaded leaders—MacDonald, Simon, Chamberlain— were Dissenters gone sour. All the same, the Dissenters of the Left were by no means so clear and decided in their opposition as they subsequently claimed. Labour in power might have done better than the Conservatives; it could hardly have done worse. It might however have repeated the Liberal experience after 1906 and aroused the Dissent of its own followers.

As a matter of fact something very like this happened in

1924. MacDonald had not been active in the U.D.C. for some time. Ponsonby and Attlee both resigned from it on taking office: 'We can truthfully say that no member of the Government is in the U.D.C.' Morel had expected to become foreign secretary. MacDonald told him that J. H. Thomas must have the office and had refused to take him as under-secretary; then MacDonald became foreign secretary himself. Morel was soon convinced that MacDonald was the prisoner of his permanent officials, like Grey before him. The affair of the Zinoviev letter, Morel held, showed 'the powerlessness of a Labour Government to control the permanent officials of the Foreign Office and to protect itself against their incapacity or worse'. MacDonald was sound on Germany from the Dissenting point of view. 'We have to see that the German people are not crushed, not enslaved, not turned into pariahs.'[1] But he was a good deal cooler towards Soviet Russia, a cause equally important to the Dissenters. He 'would stand no nonsense and no monkey tricks from Russian diplomatic representatives'.[2] The Labour government ostentatiously recognized Soviet Russia; but Mac-Donald and Ponsonby made difficulties when it came to negotiating a treaty of financial aid. On 5 August the Foreign Office actually announced that negotiations had broken down. Morel, Lansbury, and Wallhead of the I.L.P. then settled with the Russians behind the government's back and imposed their terms on it, only to have the treaty washed away in the defeat of the general election.

The second Labour government had no such troubles. Arthur Henderson emerged as 'the best foreign secretary we ever had'. Perhaps he was. But the unwonted calm had another, more practical explanation. Labour was so rent with controversy over everything else between 1929 and 1931 that it had neither time nor energy for dispute over foreign affairs. In any case the story of the two shortlived

[1] Ramsay MacDonald, *The Foreign Policy of the Labour Party* (1923), p. 22.
[2] MacDonald, *The Foreign Policy of the Labour Party*, p. 51.

minority governments is a side-issue. For most of the twenty
years between the wars the Dissenters were attached to the
official opposition. Yet they were by no means ineffective. In
one sense they achieved a success beyond their wildest
dreams. They utterly discredited 'the system of Versailles'
and, with it, all traditional diplomacy—'power-politics' as
the contemporary term of abuse had it. By the middle of the
nineteen-thirties no one dared say a word in favour of the
peacemakers of 1919; everyone paid lip-service to the League
of Nations and collective security. Yet this very success had
a disastrous outcome. The Dissenters blamed their political
opponents for the catastrophe of 1939, and with some truth;
but they themselves contributed to it. Though united and
convincing in denunciation, they never managed to formulate
a clear alternative which should satisfy the country or even
their own conscience.

   Dissent between the wars had two layers which were never
truly brought together. Its starting-point was the negative
one, handed down from Fox and Cobden, and refurbished
during the first World war by E. D. Morel. Dissenters still
assumed that foreign affairs were unnecessary. The peoples
of the world would live at peace if only they were left alone.
'No foreign politics!' was still the safest rule. England
should be reconciled with Germany and Russia; then the
world would return to its 'normal' state of permanent peace.
Morel always held this view. He never showed any interest
in 'the league of victors'. His concern was to appease Germany; and so long as he lived the Dissenters followed his
lead. His death late in 1924 marked the end of an epoch. No
single figure took his place; and the Dissenters between 1924
and 1939 were sheep without a shepherd, each puzzling his
way to an independent conclusion. The tradition which
began with Fox ended with Morel; and maybe it would
have made a tidier, more logical pattern if I had stopped at
his death. Unfortunately events go on unrolling even when
there is no one to symbolize them. In any case the Dissenters
might have pushed Morel aside once they ceased to be

content with negations. Certainly the U.D.C. soon lost its paramount influence and ceased to count as an effective force.

Dissent is, by definition, negative: it repudiates an existing Establishment. But hidden in every Dissenter is a Fifth Monarchy man, struggling to get out. The Dissenter is not content to resist present evils. He wants to see the arrival of a perfect society where nation shall speak peace unto nation; neither shall there be war any more. This had always been a strong element in Socialism. Every Socialist believed at the bottom of his heart that capitalism produced all the evils in the world; therefore Socialism would end them. The Great War strengthened this belief. Before 1914 Socialist writers assumed that the capitalist ran after money—a wicked enough thing no doubt; but it was not supposed that he loved destruction for its own sake. Indeed Brailsford and others argued that the development of capitalism made war unlikely, if not impossible. Yet a great war had come. Capitalism, being responsible for everything, was, by definition, responsible for the war. But no one could argue that war and all its terrible consequences were caused by love of wealth alone. Therefore it followed that the capitalists were 'ogres', 'cannibals' after all. These elegant phrases were the small-change of Communist writing; but all Socialists responded to them. Every new evil was laid at the door of capitalism—national antagonisms, high tariffs, political murders, moral degeneracy; and as the tale of evils mounted, so too did the conclusion that capitalists rejoiced in the sufferings of women and children. The Advisory committee of the Labour party wrote in June 1920: 'Capitalism, given over to its extreme phase of Imperialism and militarism, is shattering the material basis of civilization. . . . Our task is not to deflect the Foreign Office a little from its crazy path. Our task is to make the masses understand the ruin wrought in the world by Imperial capitalism.'

There was the rub. The last two sentences revealed the insoluble problem confronting a Utopian party which goes in for practical politics. It is no good telling the masses that they must wait for the Second Coming; the masses want things to be better here and now. Hyndman had run into this difficulty in the old days when he had insisted that there could be no amelioration of social conditions until after the social revolution. The masses had answered by turning from his Social Democratic Federation to the 'reformist' Labour party. So now it was useless to repeat: 'so long as we have capitalism, we shall have wars.' Men wanted an immediate policy of peace and security. Such a policy claimed to exist in the League of Nations. Considered in the abstract, the League was even more revolutionary than Socialism. The one demanded only a change of economic system; the other demanded a change of heart in both rulers and ruled. But this is not how the League was presented to the public. Its advocates were for the most part moderate men, respectable, high-minded; men of the Establishment, not Dissenters. Lord Robert Cecil, for example, had been Minister of Blockade during the war and was in the Conservative Cabinet until 1928; Gilbert Murray had written a pamphlet in defence of the foreign policy of Sir Edward Grey.[1] Such men claimed that the League offered all the advantages of revolution without its troubles. There need be no social upheaval, no abandonment of ancient values; simply a slight twist to the existing machine of international relations, and all would be well.

The League accorded ill with the Dissenting outlook. It demanded too much from the U.D.C.; it offered too little to the revolutionaries. Yet both groups swallowed it, though for different reasons. The isolationists of the U.D.C. could repudiate 'sectional alliances' and 'power politics' in the name of the League. Socialists accepted the League as they accepted reformism—a payment on account to be made the

---

[1] This pamphlet provoked the answer from Bertrand Russell on *The Foreign Policy of the Entente* which I have quoted earlier as one of the best statements of the Dissenting position. The argument was a family quarrel: Murray was married to Russell's first cousin.

best of until the Day of Judgement. Hence the final catastrophic paradox: Dissenters of every school put forward a
policy in which none of them believed. The League, if it
meant anything, represented an alliance of existing governments to maintain peace and security by armed strength.
Yet the U.D.C. thought that armaments were bad, and
alliances worse; the revolutionaries expected all governments to be wicked until the overthrow of capitalism. They
were all hypnotized by the doctrine of the lesser evil. Maybe
the League was wrong, but what could be put in its place?
Each group of Dissenters went on hoping that somehow it
could slip out of the tangle before it was too late. The members of the U.D.C. hoped to dodge 'sanctions'; the Socialists
hoped to avoid supporting a capitalist government. Of course
these attitudes were no worse than that of Conservatives who
'talked League' without meaning it; but they were also not
much better.

The nineteen-thirties had to wrestle with the problem:
'How do we get peace under capitalism?' and I will return
to it later. The difficulties of the U.D.C. arose much earlier.
Ramsay MacDonald defined his policy in the usual negative
terms just before taking office: 'to disestablish militarism
not merely as an organization, but as a trust. . . . Also disestablish the old methods of diplomacy which on principle
withheld information from the masses of the people . . . there
was a pronounced smack of primitive man about it.' He recognized no difference between offensive and defensive weapons:
'We have to abandon absolutely every vestige of trust in
military equipment. . . . There must be no sectional alliances,
no guarantees of a special kind.'[1] Yet his first act as foreign
secretary was to promote the Protocol, designed to stop up
the gaps in the Covenant. Mrs. Swanwick of the U.D.C., sent
as a British representative to Geneva, found that she had to
vote for a system of universal and automatic military sanctions; she did so, 'shrieking all the way'.[2] Yet shortly before

[1] Ramsay MacDonald, *The Foreign Policy of the Labour Party*, pp. 8,
20–1.   [2] Her own words to Norman Angell. N. Angell, *After All*, p. 242.

this she had signed a U.D.C. demand for 'a guarantee of mutual security through the instrumentality of an all-inclusive and reformed League of Nations'.[1]

The Conservative government jettisoned the Protocol and substituted the more limited guarantee of Locarno. This put the Labour party in a difficulty. It really disliked all guarantees, yet had to complain that the guarantee of Locarno was not universal. MacDonald merely lamented the lost moment for appeasement:

> It comes; it goes. It is always passing. It comes like a tremendous flood. The moment it reaches its maximum it begins to end [? ebb], and unless the opportunity is taken swiftly, unless you use every opportunity that that change in mind has opened up, then the harvest will never ripen, but will be like the seed sown in stony ground; it withers away before it ripens.[2] .

J. H. Hudson, supporting the Labour amendment and therefore demanding universal guarantees, said: 'If another war comes, whatever be the pretext of that war, in no circumstances will I take part by force of arms in backing up the decision that the Government has made.'[3] The Labour party conference of 1926 rejected a resolution condemning Locarno, but it also resolved that 'the workers will meet any threat of war, so-called defensive or offensive, by organizing general resistance, including the refusal to bear arms.' Arthur Henderson is supposed to have been more realistic. At the end of his life he said that disarmament had been impossible because of 'the failure to tackle security effectively before we started on disarmament'.[4] He did not take this line earlier. He said at the Labour party conference in 1929: 'We are out to end war. We are out to end the waste and folly of competitive armaments'; and he did not attempt to revive the Protocol when he became foreign secretary.

The Dissenters would have denied that there was any inconsistency in their attitude. Once accept the view that

[1] H. M. Swanwick, *Builders of Peace*, p. 1157.
[2] *Hansard*, fifth series, 188, 436.   [3] *Hansard*, fifth series, 188, 478.
[4] Norman Angell, *After All*, p. 252.

Germany was an innocent Power, and it followed that the only threat to peace came from the disparity of armed strength between her and France. Get France to disarm, and security would follow of itself. MacDonald, for instance, saw the vital part of the Protocol in the provision that it would not come into force until France and her allies had disarmed down to the German level. The British guarantee was offered solely because it would never be called on. Many an individual has landed in the bankruptcy court by making a similar assumption when he backed a bill. All that the Dissenters cared for in the League of Nations was the appeasement of Germany. They had committed themselves to this course when they denounced the settlement of Versailles; and they held to it through fair weather and foul.

The Labour party had condemned the peace settlement even before it was made. Its attitude soon received powerful reinforcement. J. M. Keynes fulfilled 'the solemn pledge' which he had made in his own mind to his Cambridge friends. Resigning from the British delegation to the peace conference, he blasted it and all its works in that epoch-making book, *The Economic Consequences of the Peace*. Claiming to write as an economist, he relied on a simple economic argument. Germany was the economic centre of the Continent; therefore anything which weakened her impoverished all Europe. He quoted the German Note against the peace terms: 'Those who sign this Treaty will sign the death warrant of many millions of German men, women and children'; and added: 'I know of no adequate answer to these words.' Keynes, I am told, was a very good economist, but there can be few examples in history of a judgement that went more astray than this condemnation of the peace settlement. Not a single man, woman or child died in Germany as a result of the peace of Versailles. Indeed the children whom it was supposed to sentence to death were the Nazi soldiers of 1940, about the toughest fighting men that the world has ever known. Keynes was also a writer of genius, combining the literary qualities of Bertrand Russell and Lytton Strachey. For every reader who followed his argument against reparations there were a thousand who appreciated the portraits of Wilson being bamboozled, Lloyd George betraying his pledges, Clemenceau in his black gloves thinking only of France. The man least affected by this rhetoric was, curiously, John Maynard Keynes. If there was a villain of sly expediency in *The Economic Consequences of the Peace*, it was Lloyd George; yet within a few years he and Keynes were the closest of associates. Or again, in October 1939 Keynes wrote to the *New Statesman*, praising Colonel Blimp and the Old School Tie, 'for whom three cheers'. Yet it was Colonel Blimp, or, to be more exact, some three hundred M.P.s, including Sir Samuel Hoare and Edward Wood, later Lord Halifax, who, by threatening to revolt, imposed on Lloyd George the harsh peace terms which Keynes condemned.

Keynes made no political comment except by implication. He attributed the faults of the peace-settlement to human stupidity and selfishness, not to the capitalist system; and he believed to the end of his life that men' would follow the sensible course sooner or later if it were pointed out to them. Other Dissenters turned Keynes's weapons in a different direction—against capitalism and against France, two evils which they seemed to regard as synonymous. Brailsford, for instance, echoed Keynes's economic prophecy:

One may sum up the Peace of Versailles in a sentence. It robbed Germany at once of the means of production, and of the motive for production. While this Treaty stands unrevised, there can be no resumption, save on the puniest scale, of the activity which, in the generation before the war, had made Germany the workshop of the Continent.[1]

He had certainly not lost that confident touch which in March 1914 led him to rule out a great European war. A further prophecy however came true in a way that he did not expect:

The image of the future . . . is that of all Central Europe

[1] H. N. Brailsford, *After the Peace* (1920), p. 21.

reduced to the condition of a camp of prisoners of war, kept at work for the benefit of their gaolers.[1]

Next Brailsford, unlike Keynes, threw in an explanation:

Our vicious capitalist system . . . crushed the most productive people . . . and showered its favours on Poles, Roumanians and Jugo-Slavs, primitive unschooled races . . . who never, even after generations of experience are likely to replace the Germans as industrial or intellectual workers.[2]

No one would guess from this that Brailsford had started life as an enthusiastic admirer of the Macedonians.

These 'primitive unschooled races' had many faults. They lacked industrial power; and now made matters worse by seeking to develop it. They maintained large armies; they failed to operate democratic government. Their independent states had come into existence 'only because the Allies . . . prolonged the war until their extreme purposes could be realized'.[3] They were condemned if they failed to observe the principle of national self-determination: 'The worst offence was the subjection of over three million Germans to Czech rule.'[4] But they were also condemned if they asserted their national claims at the expense of Germany:

A broad corridor (which happens to be largely populated by Poles) was carved out, in order that Polish munitions might . . . run from Danzig to Warsaw . . . ; it separates from the body of the German nation, like a limb severed from its trunk, the intensely German province of East Prussia.[5]

The Dissenters now levelled against 'the succession states' all the hostility which, before the war, they had felt against Russia. There was an added charge. Where previously France had been denounced as the ally of Russia, the succession states were now denounced as the ally of France. The old 'liberal alliance' went into eclipse between the peace of

[1] H. N. Brailsford, *After the Peace* (1920), p. 82.
[2] H. N. Brailsford, *After the Peace* (1920), p. 22.
[3] Brailsford, *After the Peace*, p. 49.
[4] Brailsford, *After the Peace*, p. 47.
[5] Brailsford, *Olives of Endless Age*, p. 82.

Versailles and Hitler's reoccupation of the Rhineland. France became instead 'a state, traditionally militaristic, which enjoys today a domination over Europe unequalled for a century'.[1] Brailsford, as usual, carried the idea furthest:

The relative military power of France is now vastly greater than that of Germany ever was. . . . The disparity will be permanent. . . . France has recovered the military predominance which she enjoyed under the first Napoleon.
Her partial eclipse during the last fifty years that followed Sedan has obliterated our recollection of the persistent military tradition of this most nationalist of peoples. . . . A nation of small peasant owners and small investors will never be Liberal in the British sense of the word.[2]

Though all Dissenters held these views about France, E. D. Morel took the lead in the campaign against her as he had done ever since Agadir. The French occupation of the Ruhr enabled him to repeat his successful agitation over the Congo of many years before, though now the other way round. Once he had denounced the Belgians for not treating coloured peoples as their equals; now he denounced the French for regarding coloured troops as the equals of the Germans. His pamphlet, *The Horror on the Rhine*, went through eight editions within a few months of publication. Morel visited Germany (for the first time) where he listened sympathetically to such liberal figures as Stresemann, Tirpitz, and von Kehr. On his return, Baldwin listened sympathetically to him, remarking characteristically: 'You have no idea how frightfully difficult it is to get anything done.' MacDonald said to Morel of Baldwin: 'On all essentials his views coincide pretty closely with ours. . . . Germany must be maintained as much in our interests as anything else.'

Morel's most assiduous correspondent from Germany was Montgelas, an early fighter against 'the war-guilt lie'. Montgelas wrote to him: 'We are the most peaceful nation that ever existed and never fight except when we believe that we are attacked.' Not that Morel needed much prompting.

[1] Morel, preface to *Builders of Peace*.
[2] Brailsford, *After the Peace*, pp. 70, 79.

M

His own pamphlets had already laid down the lines on which the 'scientific' study of war-origins was to proceed. One member of the U.D.C., Sir Daniel Stevenson, founded the Stevenson Chair of International History at the London School of Economics—the only such chair in the country—as part of the campaign against 'war-guilt'. Other members of the U.D.C. provided the works of history which were used at the universities for the same purpose. I can speak here from personal experience. When I went to Manchester in 1930, I found that I had to teach European history to 1914. Having been educated at Oxford, I knew none after 1878. I hastily botched together a reading list, which I turned up the other day. This is how it begins:

Bertrand Russell, *Freedom and Organization 1814–1914.*
Lowes Dickinson, *The International Anarchy.*
G. P. Gooch, *History of Europe, 1878–1914.*
H. N. Brailsford, *The War of Steel and Gold.*

All four writers were members of the U.D.C. Of foreign authors I used Erich Brandenburg, a German who kept his chair under Hitler, and Sidney Fay. As late as 1947 Fay— provoked, I am not sorry to say, by me—declared that neither later events nor all the volumes of British and French documents had led him to modify the conclusions which he had reached many years before on the basis of the German documents alone. I knew nothing of the French historians; and was lucky to escape the works of Harry Elmer Barnes. Later, a few historians tried to go against the current: Berna- dotte Schmitt in 1930 with his book on *The Coming of the War,* Woodward in 1935 with his profound study of the Anglo- German naval rivalry. To judge from the views still gene- rally held, these books might as well not have been written. The U.D.C. version of events holds the field. Attempts to shake it are dismissed as controversial, 'iconoclastic, rather than authoritative'.[1]

It would take a whole lecture to discuss this U.D.C. ver- sion in detail and to set it against the record. I will take one

[1] *English Historical Review,* lxx, 295.

instance—Lowes Dickinson, partly because his books are more readable than those of Dr. Gooch, partly because of the admiration with which intellectual circles still regard him. If you doubt whether he had any lasting influence, let me remind you that *The International Anarchy* was reprinted unchanged as late as 1938 with a flattering preface by Sir Arthur Salter; for all I know it may still be in print. Here are some of his historical judgments, taken from *War: Its Nature, Cause, and Cure* (1923). The German navy was built 'to defend her trade'—this is contradicted by the preamble to the German Navy Bill and by the writings of Tirpitz. The German government 'desired to keep the trade of Morocco open to all'—the German documents themselves show that the Germans attached no importance to Morocco (where they had virtually no trade), but planned to break the Anglo-French entente. Russia 'wanted supremacy in the Balkan Peninsula'—on the contrary she wanted it left alone. Serbia was 'primitive, barbarous, aggressive'. The secret treaties were 'the sufficient, final and irrefutable proof of the real objects of the Powers of the Entente'. The Great War 'like all international wars, had for its objects, on both sides, increase of power and seizure of territory'. As an additional curiosity, this book, devoted among other things to the cure for war, gave precisely one sentence to the League of Nations.

The campaign against 'the war-guilt lie' cut more deeply than the original protest against the peace treaties. The peace terms had been condemned as harsh, unfair, even unworkable. Nevertheless they had some moral justification if Germany was solely responsible for the outbreak of war. Once it could be shown that she was no more responsible than others, perhaps even less so—more sinned against than sinning, a 'have-not' nation kept out by the greedy 'haves'—then the moral case for the peace treaties disappeared. Many men, by no means Dissenters, found in the study of war-origins their road to Damascus. Philip Kerr, later Lord Lothian, for example, had been Lloyd George's private secretary at the Paris peace conference and, as such, had drafted the Allied answer to the German complaints. Then he had stressed Germany's war guilt. Later he picked up a book by some U.D.C. historian, and from that moment became a fanatic advocate of appeasement. Discrediting the peace treaties destroyed also the French case for security. If Germany had not deliberately planned the war, still more if (as some historians held) war had been forced on her by France and Russia, she had as much right for security against France as France had against her. For that matter, all security was unnecessary. The Great War had been merely a muddle, a mistake. Men had learnt from its horrors not to make that mistake again. They would negotiate—preferably through the machinery of the League of Nations. It is significant that the phrase 'collective security' was never used until the middle of the nineteen-thirties.

The Dissenters were mainly concerned with the hardships of Germany. But Russia was not forgotten. The years between the peace-making and the triumph of Hitler were a historical freak: it was not necessary to choose between Russia and Germany. Whoever sympathized with Germany sympathized with Russia also, and the other way round. The Bolshevik rulers saw their main enemy in 'the brigands' of the Anglo-French entente. They, too, denounced Versailles; and Soviet Russia became a 'revisionist' Power. Russian historians simply put the German case (which was also the U.D.C. case) into Russian words. Pokrovsky, for example, was as keen as Morel or any German to demonstrate the war-guilt of Poincaré and the tsar. The one novel idea was that British policy aimed at a united capitalist bloc against Soviet Russia; hence the British opposition to the occupation of the Ruhr, and British enthusiasm for Locarno. This argument could have been turned against the whole trend of appeasement, as it was a decade later. In the nineteen-twenties, the Soviet rulers assumed, like everyone else, that the Germans were the weaker of the two sides. They staved off the supposed threat of intervention by assisting the secret rearmament of Germany; and did not worry about the embarrassment that this caused to their friends in Western Europe—not that the friends of Soviet Russia are ever embarrassed for long. The Communist International, dominated by the Russians, and the revived Socialist International, under German influence, were bitter rivals; but both denounced the peace settlement in exactly the same terms. It is not surprising that all English Dissenters joined in the tune.

I shall not discuss in detail the international affairs of the nineteen-twenties. It was a decade of peace and misleading 'normalcy' despite the dramatic phrases and sometimes the dramatic events. Did even Palme Dutt believe in the capitalist war of intervention against Soviet Russia which he foretold each month in the columns of the *Labour Monthly*? Did Commander Kenworthy really think in 1928 that 'the danger of war between this country and America . . . is as real as between Germany and this country in 1906'? The decade had its importance as a period of education. The Dissenters faced the urgent problems of the nineteen-thirties with their minds made up, their ideas rigid. Everyone from respectable academics to Communist pamphleteers taught them to regard France as the centre of Imperialism and to distrust 'power-politics'. They all clung to a simple proposition: if there were no armaments, there would be no war. And they thought it their principal duty to ensure that their own country at any rate was out of the running as a belligerent. Even those who saw some good in the territorial settlement of Versailles, as Hugh Dalton did,[1] hoped that frontiers would 'fade away'.

Though ephemeral organizations constantly appeared— Anti-War Councils, Peace Committees, Aid for this country and that—none captured the predominant place as the U.D.C. had done in the great days of E. D. Morel. There were no new writers. The Dissenting voices were still those which had been raised before the first World war—Brailsford, Bertrand Russell, Norman Angell, Leonard Woolf. Now I come to think of it, there was one new writer, a host

[1] Hugh Dalton, *Towards the Peace of Nations* (1928).

in himself: Covenanter, Diplomaticus, Vigilantes (when he actually described himself as three men—he certainly wrote enough for three). It is a safe rule which I present to future researchers that anyone writing in the nineteen-thirties under a name other than his own was Konni Zilliacus, then an official of the League of Nations. He was to be labelled later a fellow-traveller, even a disguised Communist. Incorrectly. Zilliacus was simply Covenanter, a single-minded believer in the League of Nations. All his writings were variants on the same theme: 'Enforce the Covenant.' Why did the statesmen of the world not obey this admirable instruction? Here Zilliacus was content to follow the explanations of others. Sometimes he echoed E. D. Morel and the U.D.C.; sometimes he spoke like a revolutionary Marxist; sometimes he combined the two, as though Ramsay MacDonald and Lenin had written alternate sentences. In 1933 he blamed 'international anarchy'; in 1935 'the failure of human wisdom'; by 1939 he had settled on 'the Government's subservience to the interests of the plutocracy'. He wrote in 1933:

A large part is due to the personal shortcomings of Sir John Simon. . . . Another reason is the personality of the Prime Minister.

But in 1939:

The causes of the failure of the Government's foreign policy are not to seek in the personal shortcomings of this or that Minister.[1]

It might seem that Zilliacus had moved on, as other Dissenters did, from U.D.C. rationalism to Marxism. Not at all: in 1944 he was still cheerfully combining the two, denouncing 'secret diplomacy' in one breath and 'Capitalist imperialism' in the next.[2] He was in truth so convinced of the virtues of the Covenant that he never paused to inquire why others did not share his enthusiasm. This made him an unsatisfactory guide for the Dissenters. He was indifferent to the evils of Versailles—how could he condemn a treaty which enshrined the Covenant? He had no sympathy with Ger-

[1] Vigilantes, *The Dying Peace* (1933); *Inquest on Peace* (1935); *Why We are Losing the Peace* (1939).
[2] K. Zilliacus, *Mirror of the Past* (1944).

many, nor indeed with Soviet Russia, until she won his approval by joining the League in 1934. He did not worry about South Tyrol or Danzig or the Germans of Bohemia: only about Article X and Article XI and Article XVI. His writings gave no help to the Dissenters in their practical problem: how could they conduct an active policy without ceasing to be Dissenters? In more concrete terms, how could they resist Fascism without becoming the allies of British Imperialism? More concretely still, how could they fight Hitler in the name of Versailles?

The problem did not of course emerge fully grown. In 1932 Hitler was not yet in power. The Labour party, reeling under the catastrophic defeat of 1931, fell back on the pure milk of the gospel. It was unitedly convinced that all the fault lay with 'the narrow nationalism and indifference to the League of Nations of the British government'. The party would have liked to commit itself to unilateral disarmament. Henderson staved this off only by pleading that they should give the Disarmament conference a chance. He added, referring to the general strike resolution of 1926: 'If the time comes, if the necessity arises, that resolution will still be the policy of the party.' At the 1933 conference 'war-resistance' was carried without a vote. Henderson explained that collective security and war-resistance were really the same thing. Adherence to the League of Nations meant only 'the obligation to withhold all support from a Government that breaks its pledge to keep the peace . . . a common refusal to assist the international criminal who breaks the peace'.

By 1934 the ice was beginning to melt. Hitler had destroyed the German Labour movement; and the British trade unions felt strongly against him. Moreover, with the German Socialists silenced, the French had a greater influence on their British comrades, as happened during the first World war; and this strengthened the case for security. The Labour party executive presented the 1934 conference with a statement that 'this country might have to use military and naval forces in support of the League'; and it would be the duty of the party 'unflinchingly to support our Government in all the risks and consequences of fulfilling its duty to take part in collective action'. There were a few murmurs of Dissent from the pacifists. William Mellor preached the old orthodoxy: 'War arises out of capitalism itself. A Socialist government should base its policy on preserving peace . . . by a close alliance with the U.S.S.R.' One Dissenter now changed sides. Attlee said: 'It is easier to believe in unilateral disarmament when you live in England than on the continent. Ultimately we shall not get peace until we have world Socialism, but we have to deal with things as they are today.' He added rather confusingly: 'We are out for a world State . . . we are out for the abolition of armed forces. We are out for sanctions in the hands of the League.'

These discussions were still academic. The Dissenters, right up to the Labour leaders, were unshakably convinced that the National government would persist in its wickedness. They had no fear of finding themselves on its side. Support for collective security was at most a declaration of what Labour would do when returned to power. Indeed the resolutions were little more than an expression of the affection felt for Arthur Henderson. He had the Geneva bee in his bonnet; and it did no harm to let him have his way. But collective security was not regarded as encroaching at all on either disarmament or war resistance. It came to be believed later that Japan's invasion of Manchuria drew clear lines for the great debate over sanctions. This is not true. The League never condemned Japan as an aggressor.[1] Neither the Labour party nor the League of Nations Union demanded military sanctions against her. Even 'A Student of the League' who sent denunciations of the British government from Geneva to the *Manchester Guardian* only advocated the withdrawal of diplomatic representatives from Tokyo.[2] The *Manchester*

[1] In February 1933 the Assembly of the League agreed that Japan had resorted to force, contrary to her obligations under the Covenant— a different thing.

[2] 'A Student of the League' was much drawn on by Zilliacus later; an agreeable arrangement, since the Student was Zilliacus himself.

Guardian itself wrote: 'We neither wish nor expect to fight the Japanese.'[1] Even so it was criticized by Gilbert Murray for stressing the implications of the Covenant. The Labour party, rather to its own surprise, proposed an arms embargo on both China and Japan; and when the government duly enforced this, it was applauded by Lansbury, the leader of the parliamentary party, with the support of his followers. In fact if the Dissenters took any consistent line over the Manchurian affair, it was that world disapprobation would be effective in itself.[2]

Nor did the rise of Hitler shake Dissenting faith in appeasement. On the contrary, it made them more convinced than ever that Germany's grievances must be righted before it was too late. The old emotion against Versailles proved stronger than dislike of Fascism or the half-hearted conversion to collective security. Until 1936 Hitler advanced to a mounting chorus of Dissenting applause. Everything was happening just as they had foretold; and all Hitler's grievances must be met before they could think of resisting him.[3] Brailsford wrote on 3 June 1933: 'If Great Britain would remove the root causes of German hysteria by disarming and removing Germany's economic burdens, the ordinary laws of moral causation will work. She will have received justice without recourse to force.'[4] When Hitler left the Disarmament conference, the Dissenters drew the moral that further concessions should be made in order to win him back again. The Advisory Committee insisted: 'We must disarm down to the German level.'[5] The *Daily Herald* wrote: 'If the European Powers turn their backs on a policy of appeasement and on the League . . . nothing lies ahead but new and fratricidal

---

[1] 13 December 1931.
[2] The Manchurian affair is fully discussed in R. Bassett, *Democracy and Foreign Policy* (1952).
[3] Neville Chamberlain and his supporters continued to use this argument until the German occupation of Prague on 15 March 1939.
[4] This and later quotations are from S. Davis, *The British Labour Party and British Foreign Policy 1933–39.* (Thesis in the library of London University.)   [5] November 1933.

war. We cannot and will not plunge again into European intrigues, European alliances or European wars.'[1]

Opponents of the Dissenters accused them at this time of advocating disarmament to the exclusion of all else; and they were certainly tempted to do so when John Wilmot, Labour candidate at a by-election in East Fulham, turned an adverse majority of 14,000 into a victory by 5,000 in October 1933, on an undeniably pacifist 'ticket'. Yet this was really a distraction from the true Dissenting line. Before 1914 opposition to the naval estimates had been the strongest plank in Radical agitation; and the idea of giving Germany 'a place in the sun' was the affair of a few specialists. Now it was the other way round. Disarmament was offered as a consequence of appeasement, not as a policy in itself, though the Dissenters did not always make this clear. Before 1914 Radicals attributed armaments and international hostility simply to the stupidity of statesmen in every country. In 1933 the Dissenters, however mistakenly, found a rational cause for them, and one which could be removed: the failure to meet German grievances. Labour proposed to meet them. A futile hope no doubt. But at least the Dissenters urged concessions when they might have had some effect; the Conservatives made them when they had lost all purpose.

Certainly the Dissenters opposed the government's feeble attempts at rearmament; but they did so because it was not linked with any constructive policy. Edith Summerskill put this very well when she said at Putney on 26 November 1934: 'The insane piling up of armaments can only be stopped by Labour's alternative of collective security through the League of Nations.' It is puzzling at first sight that a policy which involved increased commitments should be accompanied by a demand for reducing the means with which to meet these commitments. The Dissenters gave a variety of explanations. They stressed the armed support which the fifty-one members of the League would give us, and overlooked the support which we might have to give them. Again, with an exag-

[1] 16 October 1933.

gerated recollection of the blockade during the first World war, they assumed that the League could stop an aggressor by economic means alone; and forgot that some two million Germans had to be killed as well. They also supposed that, so far as this country was concerned, war would come only in defiance of the League of Nations, never under its aegis. Hence even pacifists supported the League; generals and admirals opposed it for the sake of their professional interests, when they ought to have been its most enthusiastic adherents.

Most of all, the Dissenters relied on appeasement. They were practical men, as they always had been; not system-makers like the hot-gospellers of the Covenant from Robert Cecil to Zilliacus. They saw the danger of war in German grievances, not in some defect of Article XVI. They believed, with some justice, that there would be no general war if Germany were content; and, with less, that she would be satisfied with the destruction of 'the slave treaty'. Of course they would have liked Versailles to be revised by agreement; but better done unilaterally by Germany than not at all. They were delighted when Hitler re-established conscription: 'Europe is bright with hope. . . . Versailles is dead, and the League can live.'[1] Attlee added the usual negative: 'It is impossible for us to get any kind of security through re-armament.'[2]

The Dissenters raised their last cheer on this note for the German reoccupation of the Rhineland. They had never liked the treaty of Locarno, even though it met their condition of having received parliamentary sanction. At best they accepted it with the unspoken proviso, borrowed from the abortive Protocol, that it should come into force only when France disarmed. She had failed to do so. Hence the Dissenters felt no obligation. Brailsford wrote triumphantly: 'If danger overtakes France, it will be because she has striven to maintain the Clemenceau system of hegemony.'[3] The *Daily Herald* wrote on 9 March 1936: 'the crisis may blow more good than

<hr>

[1] *Daily Herald*, 29 March 1935. [2] *Daily Herald*, 4 April 1935.
[3] *New Statesman*, 9 May 1936.

ill'; and Arthur Greenwood found the situation 'pregnant with new and great possibilities for the future of the world'. The Advisory Committee of the Labour party thought that France might be given 'moral satisfaction' by a verdict from the Hague court. But Hitler's new offer gave 'a supreme opportunity for reversing the wheels of international policy now turning rapidly in the direction of war': Germany should be given complete equality within the League of Nations, and British rearmament should be suspended. It is, I think, a fair guess that any attempt to expel Hitler from the Rhineland would have met with united opposition from the British Labour movement—and of course from nearly everyone else in England.

Yet only the previous autumn British Labour had committed itself to collective security, and therefore to the sanctity of treaties, in dramatic circumstances. Italy's attack on Abyssinia produced the most savage controversy ever known within the ranks of the Left. All those who had given the Labour party its Dissenting character opposed sanctions, at any rate so long as the National government was in power. A few were pacifists like George Lansbury, who lost his leadership in the House of Commons over this issue. Others were old members of the U.D.C., still believers in 'peace by negotiation': Arthur Ponsonby, who resigned the leadership in the House of Lords, took this line. Not that the U.D.C. held together even now. Roden Buxton supported sanctions against Italy: Noel Buxton opposed them on the ground that there were still slaves in Abyssinia. But most of those who resisted sanctions had the Dissenting outlook which had been universal in the Labour movement until only the day before: nothing good could come from a capitalist government. Cripps said: 'Every war entered upon by a capitalist government is and must be an imperialist and capitalist war.' William Mellor put it even more simply: 'Our enemy is here.'

The supporters of sanctions claimed to be practical men. In Attlee's words, they took the world as they found it. The trade unionists, led by Ernest Bevin, regarded sanctions as the international equivalent of a strike; the former associates of Arthur Henderson had long been striving to lead the Labour movement into collective security without being caught in the act. Herbert Morrison saw in the League of Nations 'the beginning of world government'. Dalton exhorted: 'Play the part of a Great Power for peace, a Great Power for righteousness, a Great Power for Socialism, a Great Power for social justice'—it is difficult to see what all this had to do with Abyssinia. The dispute over sanctions was meant to be a turning-point. It was the moment when the Labour movement was captured from the Dissenters— liberated from them, if you like—and transformed into the alternative government, as Liberalism had been before it.

This was the intention, not the reality. The passionate debate evaded the real issue: Germany. Dissenters had never been interested in Italian grievances. None of them felt the twinge of sympathy for Mussolini that they did for Hitler. Cripps and his associates thought that the British government was wrong, not that Mussolini was right—this perversity was confined to Bernard Shaw. Besides, opposing Italy would not have led to a great war as everyone knew secretly; and for that matter the defeat of Mussolini would not have made a ha'porth of difference so far as Hitler was concerned—it might even have landed us with Italy as an ally and, heaven knows, the alliance with France nearly brought us to the ground in 1940. The Abyssinian crisis was not really a Dissenting affair at all. The leaders in it were the high-minded, not the Dissenters: the League of Nations Union, the Cecils, the Toynbees, the Gilbert Murrays, heirs of Gladstone maybe, but certainly not of Bright, still less of the Chartists. It was a repeat performance of the Bulgarian Horrors with the two Archbishops and *The Times* making a startling reappearance on the side of righteousness. The outcry against the Hoare-Laval plan came from the solid, the respectable: Austen Chamberlain in parliament, Geoffrey Dawson outside it.

There was one new element: the Communist party outdid even the League of Nations Union in its enthusiasm for collective security. The most enjoyable experience in my political life was a meeting at Manchester when I opposed sanctions against Italy before an indignant audience drawn in equal parts from the League of Nations Union and the Communist party. Until 1934 the League of Nations had been 'the league of brigands'; when Russia joined, it became an alliance of the peace-loving Powers. The Communists were the only British party to have a clear record of opposition to Hitler from 1933 to 1939, and the only party to advocate undiluted collective security. This is perhaps a point of some interest in British history, but it does not qualify them as Dissenters. They were merely supporters of a rival establishment: they did whatever the Soviet leaders told them to do. Previously they had embarrassed the Dissenters by agreeing with them; now the orthodox were embarrassed in the same way.[1] It was a great relief so far as the Dissenters were concerned. Most people were disillusioned when the Russians made the Nazi-Soviet pact in 1939; the Dissenters had been disillusioned when Soviet Russia joined the League in 1934.

When the excitement over Abyssinia died away, it became clear that Labour had failed to take the big jump after all. The Labour leaders who advocated collective security did not take the further step of proposing a coalition with the National government. They did not even establish their claim to be more effective agents of collective security. Labour candidates kept quiet about military sanctions at the general election—more from lack of faith in them than from the realization that they would lose votes. Nor did anyone suggest, during the great explosion over the Hoare-Laval plan, that Attlee should be called in to execute the will of the nation instead of Baldwin. In theory the Dissenters had been repudiated by the Labour party over Abyssinia; in practice

[1] I have a confused recollection that Winston Churchill and Harry Pollitt appeared on the same platform at a League of Nations Union meeting. Perhaps this did not happen; but it could have done.

they won. They had said that the National government could
not be trusted; and events proved them right. Attlee acknowledged the victory of the Dissenters when he put into
words the sentiments about Baldwin expressed in David
Low's cartoons: 'The people of this country trusted the right
honourable Gentleman and really believed that he stood for
peace. He wantonly threw that confidence away, and he will
not get it again.'

Labour policy thereafter had two contradictory aspects, a
contradiction not resolved until May 1940. On the one hand,
an advocacy of collective security that grew ever more
rigorous and uncompromising; on the other, a distrust of
the National government so complete as to make any active
policy impossible. One group was certainly defeated: the
advocates of 'appeasement' now lost all hold on the Labour
party, though their ideas continued to simmer no doubt in
the collective unconscious. Charles Trevelyan was the only
founder of the U.D.C. to continue active in the Labour party,
though as a 'Crippsite' Dissenter. The others could not forget so easily the evils of Versailles. Mrs. Swanwick, like
Arthur Ponsonby, denounced the Labour policy and continued to advocate 'peace by negotiation'. Roden Buxton
gave up the room at the House of Commons from which he
had advised the Labour party on foreign affairs, making a last
reappearance in July 1939 with the advice (this time to Hitler)
that 'it would be necessary to revert to a sort of secret diplomacy'[1]—a strange end to U.D.C. idealism. Once subtract the
'appeasers' from the Labour party, as happened during the
course of 1936; and the remaining contestants agreed fundamentally despite the harsh phrases which they levelled against
each other. Even the most extreme Socialist believed that
Hitler must be met by alliances and armaments; even the
most moderate admitted that this could not be done while the
National government was in power. The difference was only
in emphasis. The official leaders spoke mainly of the danger

[1] *Documents and Materials relating to the eve of the second world war,*
ii, 109.

from Hitler. The rebels said, with William Mellor: 'Our enemy is here.' But neither would have disputed the truth of the other's statement.

Each year the annual conference was asked to find a way of escape from this dilemma. Each year it failed to do so. The 1936 conference was offered a much tougher resolution than the one which had caused such conflict in 1935. 'The policy of the Labour party is to maintain such defence forces as are consistent with responsibility as a Member of the League of Nations, preservation of the people's rights and liberties, the continuance of democratic institutions, and the observance of International Law.' Dalton underlined its meaning from the chair: 'A Labour Government would be compelled to provide an increase in British armaments.' Did this mean that they would support rearmament now? The critics feared that it did. E. Pakenham (Cheltenham) said: 'They should refuse rearmament until there was an alliance with Soviet Russia and nationalization of the arms trade.' Cripps said: 'I do not object to armaments which can be controlled by the working class of the world but do we regard the British Imperialist government as our ally?' It all turned out to be a false alarm: the leaders agreed with the Dissenters. Morrison said that they did not support the existing government and that there was nothing new in the resolution. Attlee declared: 'There is no suggestion at all of supporting the Government's re-armament policy.' The party was back where it had started.

The same story was repeated in 1937. The Executive reported that 'a Labour government, until changes in the international situation caused by its advent, would be unable to reverse the present programme of rearmament'. The adoption of the Report was moved (only on the fourth day of the conference) by Clynes who brought out for the occasion the recruiting speeches that he had made during the first World war. Aneurin Bevan answered: 'He was prepared to provide whatever support is necessary to carry out a Socialist foreign policy, but not to put a sword in the hands of our enemies that may be used to cut off our heads.'[1] Both speeches were consistent with the report, though in violent conflict with each other. The dilemma was maintained to the end. The leaders, too, were Dissenters, at any rate until they got into office. Stafford Cripps sounded a rebel when he declared: 'every possible effort should be made to stop recruiting for the armed forces'; or 'Refuse to make munitions, refuse to make armaments'. But others repudiated 'bipartisanship' with equal dogmatism, though in more moderate tones:

The foreign policy of a Government is the reflection of its internal policy. Imperialism is the form which Capitalism takes in relation to other nations. . . . There is no agreement on foreign policy between a Labour Opposition and a Capitalist Government.

These words were written by Attlee in 1937 and, rather surprisingly, republished unchanged in 1949.[2] In June 1937 the parliamentary party decided henceforth to abstain during the Service estimates instead of opposing them. It thus hoped to escape the reproach of pacifism and yet to make its protest against the government's policy. The decision was taken by 45 votes against 39. Attlee, Greenwood, and Morrison all voted in the minority. Even in April 1939 the Labour party voted against conscription. There was a difference of phrase, not of spirit, between Bevan: 'We have lost, and Hitler has won'; and Attlee: 'It is very dangerous to give generals all they want.'

The Dissenters might have had an easier time of it if Hitler had been the only problem in the world. Indeed the early summer of 1936 saw the first hints of the real National government which was set up in May 1940. The Spanish civil war cut across this and made national unity impossible. The Spanish war was the Dissenters' war more truly than any other had been. For once they had no reservations. They

[1] The most curious remark at this conference was a repudiation of national states by Ernest Bevin: 'The old Austro-Hungarian Empire was economically perhaps the soundest thing that existed in Europe'—a judgment that would not have met with Hyndman's approval.
[2] C. R. Attlee, *The Labour Party in Perspective* (1937), pp. 226–7.

N

could oppose Fascism without becoming the allies of British Imperialism or defending the settlement of Versailles. On the Day of Judgement men will be asked: 'Where was the first defeat of Fascism?' Those who answer 'The Battle of Britain' will get better marks than those who say 'Moscow' or 'Stalingrad'; but those who reply 'On the Guadaljara' will go up to the highest place. If you would test the quality of a man's Dissent, ask him whether he would go to Spain while Franco rules. Thirty pieces of silver keep their meaning even when they are called cheap pesetas. The Spanish war made the Dissenters fighting men for the first time since the days of Garibaldi's Red Shirts. The sons of those who had been pacifists in the first World war fought, some of them died, in Spain. That is why there were no pacifists in the second World war as nearly as makes no odds. But though the Spanish war taught the Dissenters to fight, it also made them more hostile than ever to the National government. They demanded 'arms for Spain', not British rearmament. Things would have been different if the government had not launched the sorry farce of the Non-Intervention Committee. As it was, this strengthened the old suspicions. In Laski's words: 'By its inherent nature this Government cannot make any war that is not an imperialist war.'[1]

We may be more inclined now to be charitable towards the government's motives. Timidity, fear of a general war and of political complications in France, perhaps played a greater part than love of Fascism or concern for British investments in Spain. The Labour party was also irresolute. The 1936 conference accepted Non-Intervention, despite protests from Bevan, Charles Trevelyan, and Noel-Baker. It is curious that while the trade union leaders, Bevin and Citrine, were more resolute than the parliamentary party against Hitler and would even have accepted an unofficial coalition with the government, they pressed Non-Intervention against the majority of the parliamentarians. Herbert Morrison, for instance, always opposed Non-Intervention, and it should be

[1] *Labour Monthly*, March 1937.

remembered in his honour. The trade unionists were perhaps
more single-minded; perhaps they were restrained by the
thought of their Roman Catholic members; and all the
Labour leaders rode off on the excuse that they were keeping
Leon Blum out of trouble. Yet when every admission has
been made, when the weakness of the Labour party has been
confessed, it still remains difficult to swallow the policy of
the British government; and it was more difficult at the time.
Would British policy have been the same if Spain had produced a Left wing rebellion against a clerical-Fascist government? The Dissenters doubted it then; I doubt it still.

The Spanish war separated the Dissenters from the Establishment just when fear of Hitler was beginning to push them
together. It even separated them from the most discontented
members of the Establishment such as Churchill. Winston
Churchill was never a Dissenter despite his fierce criticism
of the government. He had none of the Dissenting scruples
against supporting British Imperialism or maintaining the
settlement of Versailles. His object was to win over the
Conservative majority, not to destroy it—no doubt the right
line in the circumstances. His attitude to the Labour party
was: 'Come over to us'; never: 'I will come over to you.'
The Dissenters estranged him by their votes against rearmament under the existing government; he estranged them
by his neutrality over Spain. Only in the spring of 1939 did
he admit his mistake when he said to an American Radical in
a brief moment of despair: 'We're all in the same lobby now.
We're all together now.'[1] A war over Spain would have
marked victory for the Dissenters. The government would
have had to accept their leadership, not the other way round.
Hence the Spanish war still did not provide an answer to the
Dissenters' problem: should they resist Hitler by supporting
British Imperialism?

There was a further problem never allowed to come to the
forefront of their minds. The Dissenters said that they would
resist Hitler wholeheartedly if the government changed its

[1] Vincent Sheean, *Between the Thunder and the Sun* (1943), p. 222.

character, or still more if Labour took its place. But would they have done so? Despite the eclipse of the U.D.C., despite the brave talk about collective security, the Dissenters could never quite forget that they had denounced German grievances long before Hitler made them his own. Danzig and the Corridor, the enforced independence of Austria, the three million Germans in Bohemia—these were not the invention of *Mein Kampf*; they had been the principal points of the condemnation which the Labour party had issued in May 1919. Even *Lebensraum*, Germany's economic domination of Europe, had been treated by J. M. Keynes as a law of nature. Dissenters always assume that superior armaments are on their side; they need to feel that superior morality is on their side as well, and it took them a long time to do so. Of course the 'National' leaders—Chamberlain, Hoare, Simon—did much worse. They succumbed to a violent attack of Dissenting conscience just when the Dissenters themselves were recovering. Still, it was difficult even for the most anti-German to argue himself out of a moral outlook twenty years deep.

The German seizure of Austria hardly raised the problem. The Austro-Fascism of Dollfuss and Schuschnigg was peculiarly abhorrent to the Labour movement—almost more abhorrent than National Socialism itself. Independent Austria had been dead since February 1934 so far as the Dissenters were concerned. Czechoslovakia was a different matter. It was the moment of moral crisis for the Dissenters, and not for them alone: hence the emotional reaction which the word 'Munich' arouses to the present day. On paper the Dissenters were all for resistance. Labour and trade union delegations waited on the Prime Minister; firm speeches were made in parliament. Yet 'stand by the Czechs' had far less fervour in it than 'arms for Spain'. The Dissenters felt that supporting Czechoslovakia was *realpolitik*—inevitable no doubt in a wicked world, but far from the moral line that they were accustomed to. Every Dissenter felt a double twinge of shame when the *New Statesman* suggested that the German Bohe-

mians should be let go to Germany—shame that the suggestion should be made, but shame also that these Germans were
in Czechoslovakia at all. No doubt Czechoslovakia was the
only democracy east of the Rhine; but this was a recent
description—previously she had been 'the vassal state' of
French Imperialism.

The uncompromising opponents of Munich were the emi-
nently respectable, men who loathed Dissent and who had
spent their lives in or near the sanctity of the Foreign Office
—Namier, Wheeler-Bennett, Toynbee, Seton-Watson; men
who knew their way to the Athenaeum, not to the derelict
premises of the 1917 Club. None of them drew the moral that
he should join the Labour party—perhaps rightly. There is a
striking illustration of this point. Everyone knows the
nauseating scene in the House of Commons when Chamberlain announced that he was meeting Hitler at Munich, and
the members rose to their feet cheering and sobbing. Who held
aloof? Seton-Watson (who was present) says Churchill,
Eden, Amery. Wheeler-Bennett says Eden left the Chamber
—no doubt so as not to have to decide whether to stand up
or sit down—Harold Nicolson kept his seat. But Dingle Foot,
himself an M.P., recently pointed out that virtually no one
moved on the Liberal or Labour benches; and this is confirmed by the contemporary account in the *Manchester
Guardian*. Wheeler-Bennett and Seton-Watson reflect accu-
rately the spirit of the time. What happened on the Labour
and the Liberal benches did not matter. The Dissenters stood
idly by. Things might have been different if a Gladstone had
led them. He would have known how to snatch Power from
this crisis—though whether the Czechs would have benefited
is a different matter. Attlee was no Gladstone—perhaps too
modest, perhaps too cautious. The hero of Munich was not
Attlee or Cripps or even Pollitt, the leader of the Communist
party. He was Duff Cooper, erstwhile champion of Baldwin,
than which conformity could go no further.

The outcome of the Munich crisis pushed the Dissenters
even more into Dissent. In so far as they had offered to

support the government, they had been made fools of; their
support had been exploited until Chamberlain and Hitler
matured their bargain. Munich was the Hoare-Laval plan
over again, only more so. Now Chamberlain and Halifax
seemed to be preparing new betrayals, new surrenders. Even
Zilliacus despaired of the Covenant and advocated war
resistance: 'It is a delusion to imagine that this Government
will ever fight for anything but the class interests of the
plutocracy.'[1] The guarantee to Poland in March 1939 did not
restore Dissenting confidence in the government. On the
contrary, it made them more suspicious than ever. Czechoslovakia had been at least a democracy with a fairly good
record in its treatment of Germans. Poland was a dictatorship, ill-treating Germans, Ukrainians and Jews. It was the
worst stumbling-block of all so far as Versailles was concerned, and had been from the first day. Why had the government made an alliance with this corrupt, wicked, feeble state
instead of with the virtuous and powerful Soviet Union? The
question answered itself. Chamberlain had guaranteed Poland
solely because she was not Soviet Russia. The Dissenters
replied that they would support the government only when it
agreed to the Russian alliance.

This policy was sustained by practical arguments: Soviet
Russia was a great military Power; her alliance was the only
means of defeating Hitler, perhaps even of checking him
without war, and so on. Yet these arguments were a gloss, a
façade. The Soviet alliance was a shibboleth, put forward in
the sure and certain hope that Chamberlain's tongue would
stumble over it—as indeed happened. The Dissenters were
confident that Chamberlain would never make an alliance
with Russia; that is why they demanded it. Their essential
condition was one that could never be fulfilled. Therefore it
still let them out, still enabled them to evade the great question, still comforted them that the question would never be
asked. An Imperialist government would never make an alliance with Russia; equally it would never go to war against

[1] Vigilantes, *Why We are Losing the Peace*, p. 187.

Germany. Therefore the Dissenters would never be faced with the problem of whether to support it. These are odd calculations, but all Englishmen were still doing the wrong sum. Chamberlain and the Dissenters alike still assumed that Hitler's next attack would be against the Soviet Union. They supposed that they were debating the question: shall we go to Russia's aid? It occurred to none of them to ask: how can we get her to come to ours?

The legend is now firmly established that the Dissenters between the wars began as dreamers and pacifists, and moved gradually towards a more realistic, tougher policy in the usual English way. Manchuria marked the first stage, Abyssinia the next, Spain the third, and so on. At each step the Labour movement became more willing to use armed force, more resolute for collective security. The process was symbolized when Bevin overthrew Lansbury in 1935. I have long accepted this legend. Reviewing the story in detachment, it seems to me untrue. The record is one of upheaval, not of evolution. Lansbury the pacifist was not typical of the old party; Bevin the realist equally unrepresentative of the new. Until 22 August 1939 the Labour movement from Right to Left retained its old principles or, if you prefer, its old illusions. It still held the outlook of Keir Hardie and E. D. Morel, of Brailsford and J. A. Hobson. No issue of principle divided Attlee from Cripps so far as foreign policy was concerned. Two simple sentences expressed it all. Imperialist capitalism was the cause of war. Socialists should oppose both war and capitalism.

The end of the story? Perhaps. Many things perished on 23 August 1939 with the announcement of the Nazi-Soviet pact. Belief in a Communist Utopia perished on the one side; hope that Hitler would destroy Bolshevism perished on the other. It would not be surprising if English Dissent, too, perished in this storm. But perhaps not. Dissent thrives on isolation; and Stalin gave the Dissenters a new zest simply by betraying them. Collective security; the rights and wrongs of the Polish Corridor; Germany as a 'have-not' nation—

these and a hundred other idealistic phrases were forgotten. The Dissenters remembered only Bright's exception in favour of 'the honour and interest of England'; though they overdid the ruthlessness in their excitement. When Greenwood insisted on war on 2 September in confused stumbling sentences, he evoked only the interest of England. Boothby had to call out: 'And honour.'

There is no stranger document of Dissent than this speech in all the record; and none so successful. At the last minute the Dissenters won. They established the claim that—despite their previous hesitations and equivocations—the war against Hitler was their war. There is clear proof. As Greenwood rose to speak, there came a cry from Leo Amery (not recorded in *Hansard* by the way)—Amery, Tariff Reformer, Imperialist, old fighter against the Boers:

SPEAK FOR ENGLAND.

An unexpected tribute to the English Dissenters. Whether deserved . . . ?

INDEX